G2 013

Scottish SECONDARY MATHEMATICS

Tom Sanaghan

Jim Pennel

Carol Munro

Carole Ford

John Dalton

James Cairns

heinemann.co.uk
✓ Free online support
✓ Useful weblinks
✓ 24 hour online ordering

01865 888058

Heinemann

Inspiring generations

Heinemann Educational Publishers
Halley Court, Jordan Hill, Oxford OX2 8EJ
Part of Harcourt Education

Heinemann is the registered trademark of
Harcourt Education Limited

First published 2005

10 09 08 07 06 05
10 9 8 7 6 5 4 3 2 1

British Library Cataloguing in Publication Data is available
from the British Library on request.

10-digit ISBN: 0 435040 16 2
13-digit ISBN: 978 0 435040 16 1

Illustrations by Gustavo Mazali
Cover design by mcc design ltd
Printed by Scotprint
Cover photo: Stock Scotland

Acknowledgements
The authors and publishers would also like to thank the following for permission to use
photographs:

p6: Digital Vision; pp9, 17, 41, 55, 97 top left, 159: Corbis; p15; John Birdsall; pp23, 97
middle right: Harcourt Education Ltd / Peter Evans; pp39, 42, 75, 93 top, 117, 164:
Alamy; pp92, 93 bottom, 95, 97 bottom three, 109, 113: iStockPhoto; pp97 top right &
middle left, 102 left: Getty Images / PhotoDisc; p101: Rex Features; p102 right: Topfoto.

The authors wish to thank Alex McKee for his assistance with the manuscript.

Contents

How to use this book

Every chapter is divided into sections.
Each section begins with a list of key points:

1.1 Writing numbers

> The position of each digit in a number is very important.

An exercise follows:

Exercise 1.1

3 Write these numbers in figures:
  (**a**) seven thousand, six hundred and fifty

  (**b**) fifteen thousand, eight hundred

At the end of the chapter is a review exercise and a summary of all the key points.

Special instructions are shown by these symbols:

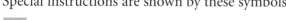 You need to use the matching numbered worksheet to answer this question.

 Use a calculator to answer these questions.

1 Whole numbers

In this chapter you will extend your knowledge of whole numbers and learn to solve problems using whole numbers.

1.1 Writing numbers

The position of each digit in a number is very important.

③46 500   The three stands for three hundred thousand.
③640 005   The three stands for three million.

It is easier to read a large number if you group the digits in threes.

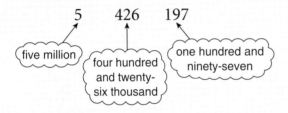

5   426   197

five million

four hundred and twenty-six thousand

one hundred and ninety-seven

One day in 2005 the population of Scotland was 5 062 011.

5   062   011.

5 million   62 thousand   and 11.

The lowest point in the Pacific Ocean is 36 198 feet below sea level (36 thousand, 1 hundred and 98).

The diameter of the sun is 1 392 140 kilometres (1 million, 392 thousand, 1 hundred and 40).

Exercise 1.1

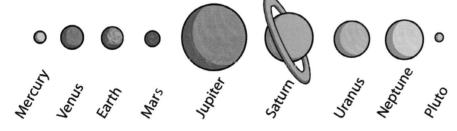

W You need Worksheet **1.1** for questions **1** and **2**.

3 Write these numbers in figures:
   (**a**) seven thousand, six hundred and fifty
   (**b**) fifteen thousand, eight hundred
   (**c**) eighty thousand, six hundred and twenty
   (**d**) four million, three hundred thousand
   (**e**) five million, seven hundred and eighty thousand, two hundred
   (**f**) six hundred and three thousand
   (**g**) one million, seven hundred and thirty-six thousand and twenty
   (**h**) two hundred and fifty thousand, four hundred and sixty-three
   (**i**) seven million, five hundred and twenty-three thousand,
       six hundred and forty.

4 Write these populations in words.

Region	Population
Highland	208 914
Edinburgh	448 624
Dundee	145 663
Dumfries and Galloway	147 765
Eilean Siar	26 502
Glasgow	577 869
Aberdeen	212 125

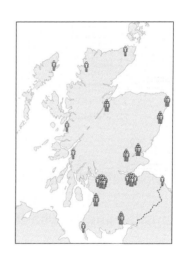

W You need Worksheet **1.2** for question **5**.

6

Planet	Mercury	Earth	Jupiter	Uranus	Venus	Mars	Saturn	Neptune	Pluto
Diameter (km)	4866	12 742	139 516	46 940	12 106	6760	116 438	45 432	2274

Write the diameter of these planets in words:
(**a**) Jupiter   (**b**) Neptune   (**c**) Mercury
(**d**) Pluto   (**e**) Mars   (**f**) Venus.

7 Write the number that is:

(**a**) 100 more than 16 483

(**b**) 100 less than 14 243

(**c**) 1000 more than 23 050

(**d**) 1000 less than 27 600

(**e**) 10 000 more than 64 000

(**f**) 10 000 less than 72 000

(**g**) 1 000 000 more than 7 800 000

(**h**) 1 000 000 less than 8 500 000

(**i**) 2000 more than 15 700

(**j**) 2000 less than 14 600.

1.2 Ordering numbers

Example

Arrange the numbers 9047, 9100, 9010, 9148, 9015, 9076 in order, smallest first.

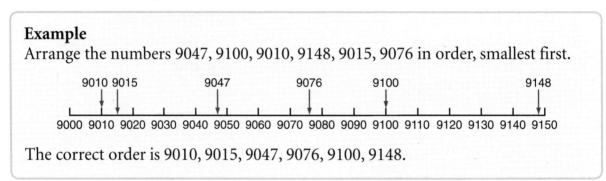

The correct order is 9010, 9015, 9047, 9076, 9100, 9148.

Exercise 1.2

W You need Worksheets **1.3** and **1.4** for questions **1** and **2**.

3 Find the missing numbers on these number lines.

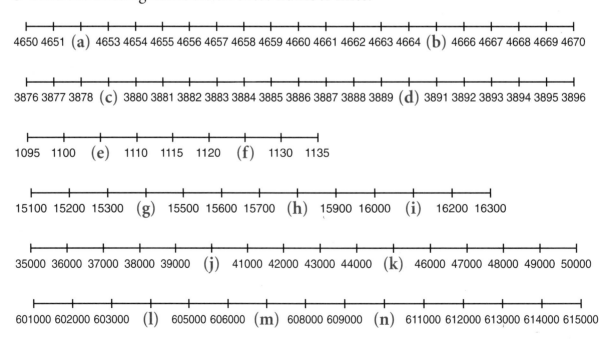

4 Write the following numbers in order, smallest first.

(**a**) 106, 150, 117, 109, 134, 143

(**b**) 2067, 2006, 2100, 2600, 2650

(**c**) 15 000, 17 100, 15 100, 15 090, 16 500, 16 093

(**d**) 240 000, 230 000, 360 000, 540 000, 340 000

(**e**) 847 000, 847 900, 846 300, 846 372, 850 000

(**f**) 107 000, 110 000, 127 000, 108 500, 107 300, 113 650

5 Potter's Pots sends bills to companies and files copies by their bill number. Arrange these bills in order, smallest first.

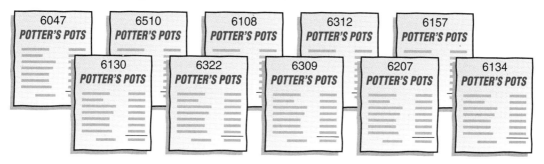

6 Arrange these planets in order of diameter, smallest first.

Planet	Mercury	Earth	Jupiter	Uranus	Venus	Mars	Saturn	Neptune	Pluto
Diameter (km)	4866	12 742	139 516	46 940	12 106	6760	116 438	45 432	2274

7 Arrange the heights of these mountains in order, smallest first.

Mountain	Height (feet)
An Socach	3018
Ben Lawers	3983
Ben Nevis	4409
Lochnagar	3789
Ben Vorlich	3093
Ben Lomond	3196
Bynack More	3576

8 Arrange these populations in order, smallest first.

Region	Population
Highland	208 914
Aberdeenshire	226 871
East Ayrshire	120 235
Glasgow	577 869
Borders	106 764
Clackmannanshire	48 077
Eilean Siar	26 502

9 The European Nations' football committee has to decide where to hold matches. By ordering the stadium capacities, find the most suitable stadium for each match.

Match	Expected attendance	Stadium capacity	
Scotland *v* France	52 500	Fir Park	13 742
Spain *v* Portugal	49 100	Celtic Park	60 294
England *v* Poland	12 500	McDiarmid Park	10 673
Germany *v* Holland	10 100	Tynecastle	17 990
Italy *v* Denmark	17 600	Pittodrie	22 199
Czech Republic *v* Estonia	14 300	Ibrox	50 411

1.3 Rounding

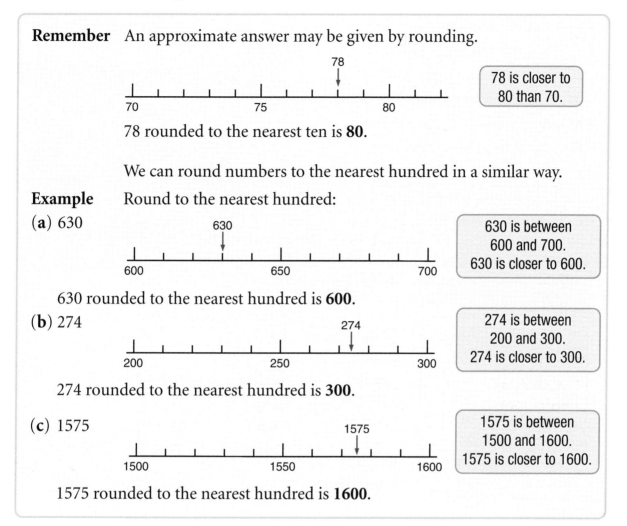

Remember An approximate answer may be given by rounding.

78 rounded to the nearest ten is **80**.

> 78 is closer to 80 than 70.

We can round numbers to the nearest hundred in a similar way.

Example Round to the nearest hundred:

(**a**) 630

630 rounded to the nearest hundred is **600**.

> 630 is between 600 and 700.
> 630 is closer to 600.

(**b**) 274

274 rounded to the nearest hundred is **300**.

> 274 is between 200 and 300.
> 274 is closer to 300.

(**c**) 1575

1575 rounded to the nearest hundred is **1600**.

> 1575 is between 1500 and 1600.
> 1575 is closer to 1600.

Exercise 1.3

1 Round each number to the nearest ten.

> For numbers ending in 5 it is common to round up.

(**a**) 47   (**b**) 13   (**c**) 86   (**d**) 49   (**e**) 99
(**f**) 241   (**g**) 386   (**h**) 207   (**i**) 4893   (**j**) 6475

You need Worksheet **1.5** for question **2**.

3 Round each number to the nearest hundred.

(**a**) 430   (**b**) 680   (**c**) 590   (**d**) 170
(**e**) 246   (**f**) 385   (**g**) 719   (**h**) 452
(**i**) 736   (**j**) 1325   (**k**) 4670   (**l**) 3206
(**m**) 6008   (**n**) 2572   (**o**) 2618   (**p**) 4427
(**q**) 86   (**r**) 22 096 (**s**) 37 555 (**t**) 20 045

4 Round each distance
to the nearest 100 km.

(**a**) Edinburgh to London, 656 km

(**b**) Paris to Madrid, 1265 km

(**c**) Rome to Vienna, 1168 km

(**d**) Prague to Copenhagen, 1033 km

(**e**) Amsterdam to Paris, 577 km

(**f**) Lisbon to Madrid, 635 km

(**g**) Milan to Rome, 689 km

(**h**) Paris to Munich, 827 km

(**i**) Copenhagen to Paris, 1329 km

5 Round each population to the nearest hundred.

Town	Population
Willing	1467
Wirt	1158
Barker	2627
Binghamton	4839
Colesville	5304
Conklin	5896
Dickinson	5121
Fenton	6792
Kirkwood	5809

Town	Population
Lisle	2340
Maine	5300
Nanticoke	1740
Sanford	2387
Triangle	2865
Windsor	6077
Allegany	8524
Ward	342
West Almond	285

6 Round each height to the nearest:

(**a**) ten   (**b**) hundred.

Munro	Height (feet)
An Socach	3018
Ben Lawers	3983
Ben Nevis	4409
Lochnagar	3789
Ben Vorlich	3093
Ben Lomond	3196
Bynack More	3576
Devil's Point	3294
Creag Mhor	3218
Ben Chonzie	3055

W You need Worksheet **1.6** for question **7**.

1.4 Addition and subtraction

Rounding helps estimate answers to our calculations.

Example 1

Janie buys a £52 coat. She is given a £19 discount because the coat is damaged. How much will she pay for the coat?

$$52 - 19$$

Estimate:	Calculate:
50	52
− 20	− 19
30	33

The coat will cost **£33**.

Example 2

Alex buys a sofa for £478 and a chair for £288. How much will he pay in total?

$$478 + 288$$

Estimate:	Calculate:
500	478
+ 300	+ 288
800	766

He will pay **£766** in total.

Exercise 1.4

W You need Worksheet **1.7** for questions **1** and **2**.

For each question in this exercise, make an estimate before you calculate the exact answer.

3 (**a**) 56 + 37   (**b**) 59 − 25   (**c**) 427 + 386
   (**d**) 89 − 36   (**e**) 126 − 23   (**f**) 244 + 139

4 (**a**) 680 − 327   (**b**) 430 + 180   (**c**) 650 − 190
   (**d**) 5130 − 3950   (**e**) 3000 − 256   (**f**) 2478 + 1334

5 Mr Forbes buys an antique clock for £265. After repairing it, he sells it for £720. How much profit did he make?

6 A freezer costs £625. If a £140 discount is given, what is the new cost of the freezer?

7 Mr Denver orders 2600 cubic metres of compost. He uses 1089 cubic metres. How much has he left?

8 An aeroplane journey across the Atlantic is 6250 kilometres.
After 3 hours, the aeroplane has travelled 1840 kilometres.
How far has it still to go?

9 Each month, Karen pays the following bills:

Mortgage – £283   Insurance – £46   Council tax – £86

How much does she pay in total?

10 To travel from Edinburgh to Sydney in Australia, Jenna flies
550 kilometres to London, then 13 000 kilometres from London
to Hong Kong, then 8500 kilometres from Hong Kong to Sydney.
How far does she travel in total?

11 Mr and Mrs Paxton are calculating the cost of carpeting
their new house.

Living room – £476
Dining room – £347
Bedroom – £186

What is the total cost?

12 Calculate the new cost of each item if the discount shown is given.

(**a**)

Camera £499
Discount £145

(**b**)

DVD recorder £509
Discount £98

(**c**)

Freezer £625
Discount £135

13 John had a coil of rope 5000 centimetres long. From it, he
cut lengths of 1500 centimetres and 2650 centimetres.

(**a**) How much rope did he cut in total?

(**b**) How much rope was left?

14 Rachel buys a suit costing £220. She receives a discount
of £50 and uses £45 worth of gift vouchers.
How much does she still have to pay?

1.5 Multiplication

I need 7 bags of cement. What will that weigh, if each bag is 45 kg?

$$
\begin{array}{r}
45 \\
\times\ 7 \\
\hline
315 \\
3 \\
\end{array}
$$

The cement will weigh **315 kilogrammes.**

Exercise 1.5

1 Copy and complete:

(**a**) $\begin{array}{r} 27 \\ \times\ 5 \\ \hline \end{array}$ (**b**) $\begin{array}{r} 18 \\ \times\ 4 \\ \hline \end{array}$ (**c**) $\begin{array}{r} 72 \\ \times\ 7 \\ \hline \end{array}$

(**d**) $\begin{array}{r} 49 \\ \times\ 6 \\ \hline \end{array}$ (**e**) $\begin{array}{r} 67 \\ \times\ 3 \\ \hline \end{array}$ (**f**) $\begin{array}{r} 126 \\ \times\ 2 \\ \hline \end{array}$

2 Calculate:

(**a**) 215×3 (**b**) 157×5 (**c**) 260×7

(**d**) 207×4 (**e**) 320×6 (**f**) 342×8

3 Linda pays £124 council tax every month. How much will 5 months' council tax cost?

4 A double decker bus carries 72 people. If a school hires 8 buses, how many people can they carry?

5 How much of each ingredient would be needed to make 7 almond cakes?

Almond Cake

(Makes 1 cake)

350 g flour
85 g ground almonds
175 g sugar
3 eggs
125 ml milk

6 (**a**) What is the cost of a room for a night at the Roxberry Hotel?

(**b**) What is the cost for 3 nights at Braemoir?

(**c**) What is the cost for 6 nights at Scobo Castle?

(**d**) The Walter family want to book 2 rooms at Inverbrochy Castle for one night. How much will this cost?

Hotel	Price per room per night
Scobo Castle	£249
Glenbeagles	£218
Braemoir	£165
Roxberry Hotel	£192
Inverbrochy Castle	£176
Ballachully Hotel	£325

(**e**) Which is cheaper, 3 nights at the Ballachully Hotel or 4 nights at Glenbeagles?

7 (**a**) How much is 7 nights at the Grand Playa for 1 person?

(**b**) What is the cost for 7 nights for 3 people at the Neptune?

(**c**) What is the cost for 4 people for a fortnight at Sun Mountain?

Hotel	Price per person	
	7 nights	14 nights
Neptune	£157	£250
El Dorado	£165	£285
Grand Playa	£183	£294
Sun Mountain	£206	£320

8 Maria buys a computer from a catalogue. She pays 9 instalments of £127 each. How much is this?

9 The monthly car parking charge in North Street car park is £8 per car. If 736 cars use the car park each month, what will the takings be for one month?

1.6 Multiplying by 10 and 100

To multiply a number by 10, you move every digit one place to the left.

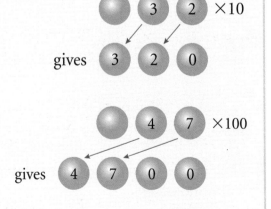

To multiply a number by 100, you move every digit two places to the left.

Example

(**a**) 56 × 10 = **560** (**b**) 134 × 10 = **1340**

(**c**) 17 × 100 = **1700** (**d**) 308 × 100 = **30 800**

Exercise 1.6

1 Calculate:
   (**a**) 15×10 (**b**) 36×10 (**c**) 153×10
   (**d**) 204×10 (**e**) 1706×10 (**f**) 500×10

2 Calculate:
   (**a**) 36×100 (**b**) 807×100 (**c**) 196×100
   (**d**) 6000×100 (**e**) 1030×100 (**f**) 47×100

3 Calculate:
   (**a**) 286×10 (**b**) 34×100 (**c**) 207×100
   (**d**) 310×100 (**e**) 1999×10 (**f**) 5030×10

4 Mixed spice is sold in 10-gramme packets. Find the weight of:
   (**a**) 15 packets   (**b**) 156 packets   (**c**) 3500 packets.

5 There are 10 millimetres in 1 centimetre.
   How many millimetres are in:
   (**a**) 3 cm   (**b**) 12 cm
   (**c**) 87 cm   (**d**) 283 cm?

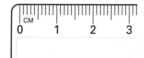

6 There are 100 centimetres in 1 metre.
   How many centimetres are in:
   (**a**) 40 m   (**b**) 136 m   (**c**) 500 m   (**d**) 736 m?

7 Irene pays her council tax over 10 months.
   If she pays £165 each month, how much does she pay altogether?

8 In an office building 294 people each donated £10 to a charity appeal.
   How much did they donate altogether?

9 Jenny saves £100 every month.
   How much will she have saved after:
   (**a**) 54 months   (**b**) 128 months
   (**c**) 306 months   (**d**) 3 years?

10 At the bank Katy can change £1 for 10 Hong Kong dollars.
   How many dollars would she receive for:
   (**a**) £45   (**b**) £500
   (**c**) £680   (**d**) £1000?

1.7 Division

If Mike has 96 CDs and each shelf holds 8, how many shelves could he fill?

$$\begin{array}{r} 1\ 2 \\ 8\overline{)9^16} \end{array}$$

He could fill **12 shelves.**

Exercise 1.7

1 Copy and complete:

   (**a**) $3\overline{)42}$ (**b**) $2\overline{)76}$ (**c**) $4\overline{)64}$

   (**d**) $5\overline{)105}$ (**e**) $3\overline{)132}$ (**f**) $5\overline{)160}$

2 Calculate:

   (**a**) $144 \div 6$ (**b**) $238 \div 7$ (**c**) $343 \div 7$

   (**d**) $375 \div 5$ (**e**) $332 \div 4$ (**f**) $674 \div 2$

3 £6500 is shared equally among 4 people. How much does each receive?

4 A farmer makes a square enclosure for sheep using 156 metres of fencing. How long is one edge of the pen?

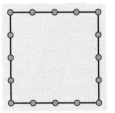

5 The £3600 profit from a charity raffle is to be shared equally among 6 charities. How much will each receive?

6 2600 apples are to be split equally into 8 boxes. How many apples will be in each box?

7 On a school trip, 145 pupils are split into 5 equal groups. How many are in each group?

8 How much of each ingredient is needed to make 1 muffin?

Muffins

(Makes 6 muffins)

420 g flour
90 g butter
150 g sugar

9 Find the cost for 1 night on each of these holidays.

CORFU **5 nights £485**	**KOS** **3 nights £282**	**PRAGUE** **7 nights £602**

1.8 Dividing by 10 and 100

To divide a number by 10, you move every digit one place to the right.

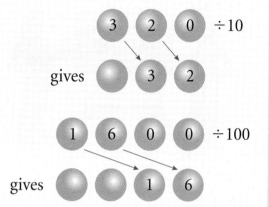

To divide a number by 100, you move every digit two places to the right.

Example

(a) $980 \div 10 = \mathbf{98}$ (b) $2010 \div 10 = \mathbf{201}$

(c) $7400 \div 100 = \mathbf{74}$ (d) $600 \div 100 = \mathbf{6}$

Exercise 1.8

1 Find:
  (a) $470 \div 10$ (b) $360 \div 10$ (c) $520 \div 10$
  (d) $8000 \div 10$ (e) $2400 \div 10$ (f) $38\,000 \div 10$

2 Find:
  (a) $1600 \div 100$ (b) $2300 \div 100$ (c) $3300 \div 100$
  (d) $4200 \div 100$ (e) $64\,000 \div 100$ (f) $50\,000 \div 100$

3 Find:
  (a) $270 \div 10$ (b) $5200 \div 100$ (c) $7200 \div 10$
  (d) $6000 \div 100$ (e) $27\,400 \div 10$ (f) $35\,000 \div 100$

4 One hundred bricks weigh 200 kilogrammes in total.
   Find the weight of one brick.

5 On a school trip 250 pupils are split into groups of ten.
   How many groups will there be?

6 Alex needs to save 10 vouchers to get one free DVD.
   If he saves 120 vouchers, how many DVDs should he receive?

7 Mr Alexander pays £1020 council tax in ten monthly instalments.
How much is each instalment?

1.9 The order of operations

I think the answer is 14.

I think the answer is 10.

$4 + 3 \times 2$

Multiply and divide before adding and subtracting.

The correct answer is **10.**

Exercise 1.9

1 Find:
(**a**) $2 + 5 \times 3$ (**b**) $3 \times 2 + 1$ (**c**) $4 + 10 \times 3$
(**d**) $4 \times 3 + 8$ (**e**) $5 + 2 \times 6$ (**f**) $5 \times 3 - 2$
(**g**) $14 - 3 \times 2$ (**h**) $4 \times 6 - 5$ (**i**) $30 \div 5 + 2$
(**j**) $16 + 4 \div 2$ (**k**) $40 \div 8 - 2$ (**l**) $20 + 9 \div 3$

2 Copy and complete using $+, -, \times$ or $\div$:
(**a**) $4 \, \square \, 3 + 2 = 14$ (**b**) $10 + 3 \, \square \, 2 = 16$
(**c**) $20 \, \square \, 2 + 3 = 13$ (**d**) $4 \, \square \, 5 - 7 = 13$
(**e**) $2 \, \square \, 4 \, \square \, 3 = 14$ (**f**) $5 \, \square \, 5 \, \square \, 1 = 26$

1.10 Making sense of answers

Stephanie needs 37 tiles to tile her bathroom.
If she can buy tiles in packs of 5,
how many packs will she need?

$$\begin{array}{r} 7 \, r \, 2 \\ 5\overline{)37} \end{array}$$

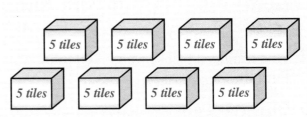

7 packs contain 35.
8 packs contain 40. $40 - 37 = 3$

Stephanie needs **8 packs.** She will have 3 extra tiles.

Exercise 1.10

1 Alice has 36 pencils.
She puts them into boxes of 5.
How many boxes will she need?

2 A lift can hold 6 people.
How many trips will be needed to take a group of 34 people?

3 Jenny has £17. She sees wooden puzzles costing £3 each.
How many could she buy?

4 Donald needs 46 tiles.
(**a**) If he can buy tiles in packs of 10, how many packs will he need?
(**b**) How many extra tiles will he have?

5 Bill's hardback books are 5 centimetres wide.
(**a**) How many books will he be able to fit onto a
shelf 83 centimetres long?
(**b**) How much space is left?

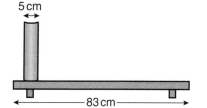

6 Mrs Robinson has 25 eggs.
(**a**) If one sponge cake uses 3 eggs, how many
sponge cakes will she be able to make?
(**b**) How many eggs will be left?

1.11 Mental strategies

Exercise 1.11

1 Find mentally:
(**a**) 36 + 25   (**b**) 27 + 15   (**c**) 18 + 23
(**d**) 16 + 18   (**e**) 35 + 26   (**f**) 43 + 58
(**g**) 84 + 34   (**h**) 72 + 19   (**i**) 75 + 47

2 Find mentally:

(**a**) 37 − 25   (**b**) 40 − 15   (**c**) 36 − 27

(**d**) 42 − 16   (**e**) 28 − 19   (**f**) 43 − 28

(**g**) 53 − 35   (**h**) 72 − 27   (**i**) 65 − 46

3 Anna buys two magazines, one costing 43 pence and the other 48 pence. How much did she spend altogether?

4 Alex buys a packet of crisps costing 23 pence.
If he hands over 50 pence, how much change will he receive?

5 Veronica orders 56 copies of the Good Home magazine for her shop.
If she sells 39 copies, how many will she have to return?

6 Juanita has a piece of fuse wire 83 centimetres long.
If she uses 27 centimetres of the wire, how much will she have left?

Review exercise 1

1 Write these numbers in figures:

(**a**) six thousand, two hundred and fifty

(**b**) twenty-four thousand, seven hundred

(**c**) forty-one thousand, six hundred and thirty-four

(**d**) four million, eight hundred and thirty-six thousand.

2 Arrange the following numbers in order, smallest first.

(**a**) 104, 120, 114, 108, 136, 154

(**b**) 3012, 3057, 3004, 3020, 3036

(**c**) 12 005, 14 100, 14 600, 13 090, 12 400, 13 093

(**d**) 216 153, 216 012, 216 200, 216 040, 216 000

3 Round the following numbers to the nearest hundred:

(**a**) 520   (**b**) 160   (**c**) 470   (**d**) 294

(**e**) 137   (**f**) 679   (**g**) 1257   (**h**) 2340

4 Copy and complete:

(**a**) $\begin{array}{r} 34 \\ \times\ 8 \\ \hline \end{array}$ (**b**) $\begin{array}{r} 127 \\ +\ 209 \\ \hline \end{array}$ (**c**) $6\overline{)282}$ (**d**) $\begin{array}{r} 767 \\ -\ 345 \\ \hline \end{array}$

(**e**) $\begin{array}{r} 478 \\ +\ 258 \\ \hline \end{array}$ (**f**) $\begin{array}{r} 234 \\ \times\ \ \ 5 \\ \hline \end{array}$ (**g**) $\begin{array}{r} 638 \\ -\ 87 \\ \hline \end{array}$ (**h**) $7\overline{)238}$

5 An internet site offers free postage when you spend over £95.
Which of these bills will receive free postage?

(**a**)
AZAZONE.COM

━━━━ £27
━━━━ £56
Total

(**b**)
AZAZONE.COM
━━━━ £32
━━━━ £29
━━━━ £37
Total

(**c**)
AZAZONE.COM
━━━━ £42
━━━━ £ 9
━━━━ £27
Total

6 Farmer Fred took 228 cattle to auction.
If 144 were sold, how many were not sold?

7 John wants to buy a car costing £7955.
If he is given a £680 discount, how much will he pay for
the car?

8 Find:
(**a**) 27 × 10   (**b**) 50 × 100   (**c**) 305 × 100
(**d**) 314 × 100   (**e**) 260 × 10   (**f**) 3506 × 10

9 Find:
(**a**) 260 ÷ 10   (**b**) 4600 ÷ 100   (**c**) 3800 ÷ 10
(**d**) 7000 ÷ 100   (**e**) 71 400 ÷ 10   (**f**) 95 000 ÷ 100

10 Jane wants to invite 56 people to her wedding.
If the hotel has tables that seat 6 people, how many tables will be needed?

11 Ryan is putting books onto a shelf.
Each book is 3 centimetres wide and the shelf is 125 centimetres long.
(**a**) How many books will fit onto the shelf?
(**b**) How much space is left?

12 A box contains 16 packs of biscuits.
(**a**) Shifty Sandwiches order 7 boxes of biscuits.
How many packs is this?
(**b**) If each pack contains 8 biscuits, how many biscuits
were ordered?

Summary

Place value

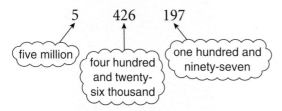

The three stands for three hundred thousand.

The three stands for three million.

630 is between
600 and 700.
630 is closer to 600.

It is easier to read a large number if you group the digits in threes.

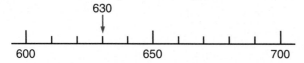

five million

four hundred
and twenty-
six thousand

one hundred and
ninety-seven

Round to the nearest hundred

Round 630 to the nearest hundred:

630 rounded to the nearest hundred is **600**.

Multiplying by 10 and 100

32×10 47×100

gives   gives

Dividing by 10 and 100

$320 \div 10$ $1600 \div 100$

gives   gives

2 Coordinates

In this chapter you will review how to read and plot coordinates.

You will learn how to find distances along gridlines, and how to give directions for a journey.

2.1 Reading coordinates

Remember   The position of a point may be described by its **coordinates**.

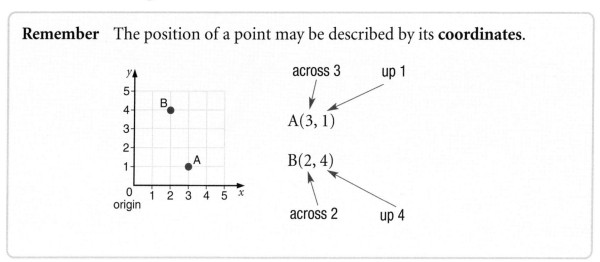

Exercise 2.1

W You need Worksheet **2.1** for questions **1** and **2**.

3 Write the coordinates of each point.

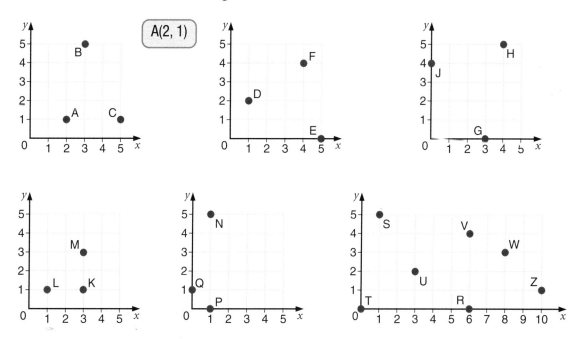

2.2 Plotting coordinates

Remember Marking a point on a coordinate diagram is called **plotting** a point.

To plot (2, 5) start from the origin,
count along 2, then up 5.

Exercise 2.2

Number the lines
carefully, as shown.

W You need Worksheets **2.2** and **2.3** for questions **1** to **6**.

7 (a) Copy the coordinate diagram.
   (b) Plot the points A(1, 2), B(1, 5), C(5, 5) and D(5, 2).
   (c) Join the points in order.
       Write the name of the shape.
   (d) What is the length of side AB?

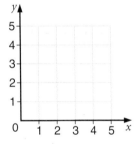

8 (a) Copy the diagram.
   (b) Plot the points E(0, 1), F(5, 1) and G(0, 5).
   (c) Join the points in order.
       Name the shape.
   (d) What is the length of the line joining the points E and G?
   (e) What is the length of line EF?

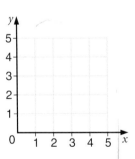

9 (a) Copy the diagram.
   (b) Plot the points H(0, 3), I(4, 3) and J(4, 5).
   (c) Write the coordinates of K so that HIJK is a rectangle.
   (d) Write the length of:
       (i) IJ
       (ii) JK.

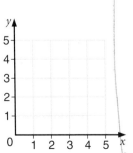

10 A shape has corners A(1, 2), B(1, 5), C(3, 7), D(5, 5) and E(5, 1).

  (**a**) What is the largest coordinate?

  (**b**) Draw a coordinate diagram large enough to
      plot these points.

  (**c**) Plot the points ABCD on your diagram, join them
      up and name the shape.

> The axes go up to the value of the largest coordinate.

11 Draw a coordinate diagram for each set of points,
  plot the points and join them in order. Name the object.

  (**a**) (6, 0), (6, 2), (5, 2), (5, 6), (4, 8), (3, 6),
      (3, 2), (2, 2), (2, 0), (6, 0)

  (**b**) (2, 6), (0, 2), (4, 2), (9, 5), (7, 9), (2, 6), (4, 2)

  (**c**) (0, 1), (1, 0), (5, 4), (5, 1), (6, 2), (7, 4), (6, 6), (4, 7),
      (1, 5), (4, 5), (0, 1)

  (**d**) (1, 0), (9, 0), (10, 1), (8, 1), (8, 3), (7, 3), (7, 5), (6, 5),
      (6, 3), (3, 3), (3, 1), (0, 1), (1, 0)

> Use the largest coordinate to decide the length of the axes.

W You need Worksheet **2.4** for question **12**.

2.3 Directions for a journey

Directions may be given to describe a journey.

Example   Describe the shaded journey along the garden path to the shed.

Start.

Go forward 2 squares.

Turn right.

Go forward 3 squares.

Turn left.

Forward 3 squares.

Turn left.

Forward 2 squares.

Turn right.

Forward 1 square.

End.

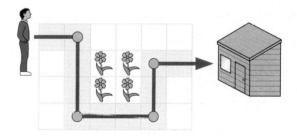

Exercise 2.3

W You need Worksheet **2.5** for questions **1** and **2**.

3 Describe each journey.

(**a**)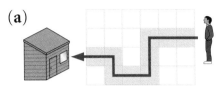

(**b**)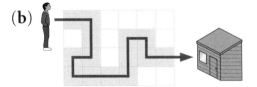

4 On squared paper, draw the journey described.

From the start position,
go forward 5 squares. Turn left.
Forward 2 squares. Turn left.
Forward 3 squares. Turn right.
Forward 3 squares. Turn right.
Forward 2 squares. Turn left.
Forward 1 square, then end.

W You need Worksheet **2.6** for question **5**.

Review exercise 2

1 Write the coordinates of each point.

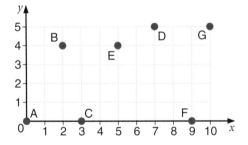

2 Look at the diagram shown.
Write the coordinates of:
   (**a**) Joe   (**b**) John
   (**c**) Frank   (**d**) Paul
   (**e**) Tom   (**f**) Carole
   (**g**) Yemi   (**h**) Jim
   (**i**) James   (**j**) Matt
   (**k**) Mathew   (**l**) Ella
   (**m**) Holly   (**n**) Mark.

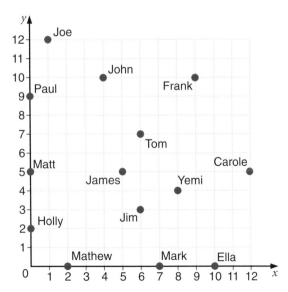

3 Copy the coordinate diagram.

Plot the points A(7, 6), B(3, 0), C(0, 2), D(11, 5), E(4, 4) and F(9, 3).

> Number the lines carefully, as shown.

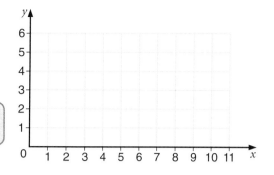

4 Copy the diagram.

(**a**) Plot the points P(4, 0), Q(0, 2) and R(4, 5).

(**b**) Join the points in order and name the shape.

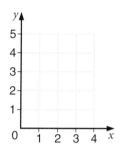

5 Copy the diagram.

Plot the points, then join them in order and name the object.

(6, 2), (6, 5), (0, 2), (9, 2), (7, 0), (1, 0), (0, 2)

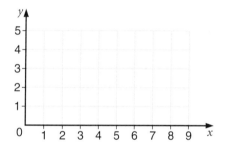

6 Copy the diagram.

(**a**) Plot the points P(1, 0), Q(0, 1), R(0, 2), S(1, 3), T(2, 3), U(3, 2), V(3, 1) and W(2, 0).

(**b**) Join the points in order and name the shape.

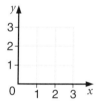

7 Copy the diagram.

(**a**) Plot the points:
A(9, 2), B(0, 2) and C(0, 5).

(**b**) Plot D so that ABCD is a rectangle.

(**c**) Write the coordinates of D.

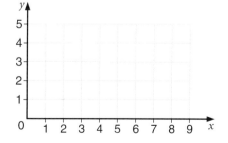

8 Describe the journey shown.

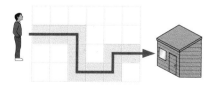

Summary

The position of a point is described by its **coordinates**.

A has coordinates (3, 1).

B has coordinates (2, 5).

Remember, from the origin count **along**, then **up**.

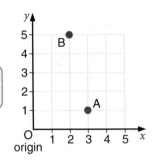

Marking points on a coordinate diagram is called **plotting** points.

A journey may be described by directions on a grid.

3 Decimals

In this chapter you will learn to use decimal fractions and solve problems using them.

3.1 Tenths

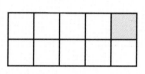
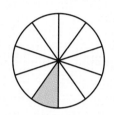

- In each of these shapes $\frac{1}{10}$ is shaded.

  As a decimal fraction, this is written 0·1

  0·1 is the same as $\frac{1}{10}$.

- In this shape $\frac{3}{10}$ is shaded.

  As a decimal fraction, this is written 0·3

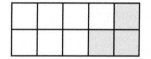

  0·3 is the same as $\frac{3}{10}$.

- 2 whole circles and $\frac{7}{10}$ of a circle are shaded.

  This is written as 2·7

Exercise 3.1

 You need Worksheets **3.1**, **3.2** and **3.3** for questions **1** to **3**.

4 Write the number represented by the shaded part in each picture.

(a)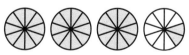

(b)

(c)

(d)

(e)

(f)

(g)

(h)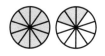

5 For each picture, write the shaded part as a decimal fraction.

(a) 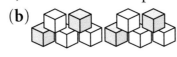   (b)    (c)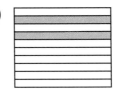

(d) 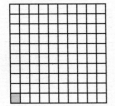   (e) 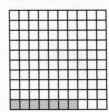   (f)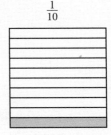

6 For each pair, write which number is bigger.

(a) 0·7 or 0·1   (b) 0·3 or 0·2   (c) 0·5 or 0·8
(d) 0·2 or 0·6   (e) 0·4 or 0·6   (f) 0·9 or 0·7
(g) 0·3 or 0·7   (h) 0·8 or 0·5   (i) 0·1 or 0·2

3.2 Hundredths

- In this shape $\frac{1}{100}$ is shaded.
  As a decimal fraction, this is written 0·01

- In this shape $\frac{7}{100}$ is shaded.
  As a decimal fraction, this is written 0·07

$\frac{10}{100}$ is the same as $\frac{1}{10}$

0·10   is the same as   0·1

- In this shape $\frac{28}{100}$ is shaded.
  As a decimal fraction, this is written 0·28

- In this shape $\frac{87}{100}$ is shaded.
  As a decimal fraction, this is written 0·87

Exercise 3.2

W You need Worksheets **3.4** and **3.5** for questions **1** and **2**.

3 Write the number represented by the shaded part in each picture.

(a)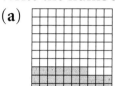

(b)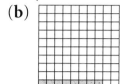

(c)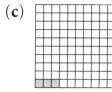

(d)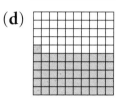

(e)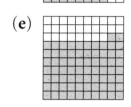

(f)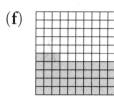

(g)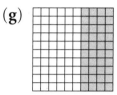

(h)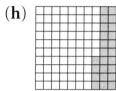

(i)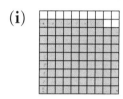

(j)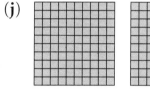

(k)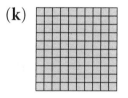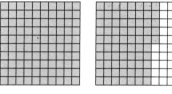

(l)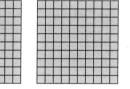

(m)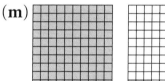

3.3 Place value

You have already seen the place value for whole numbers.
This can be extended for decimals.

H	T	U	·	Tths	Hths	
		7	·	6		This number has one decimal place.
		3	·	2	5	This number has two decimal places.
	1	4	·	3	0	This number has two decimal places.

26·47

| The 2 stands for 2 tens. | The 6 stands for 6 units. | The 4 stands for 4 tenths. | The 7 stands for 7 hundredths. |

Exercise 3.3

1 What does the digit 8 stand for in each number?

   (**a**) 0·8   (**b**) 0·08   (**c**) 0·18   (**d**) 8·04

   (**e**) 12·86   (**f**) 9·80   (**g**) 80·17   (**h**) 12·86

2 How many decimal places do each of these numbers have?

   (**a**) 45·7   (**b**) 34·31   (**c**) 15·06   (**d**) 1·4

   (**e**) 12·40   (**f**) 5·06   (**g**) 1·0   (**h**) 100·07

W You need Worksheets **3.6** and **3.7** for questions **3** to **6**.

7 Write the value of each letter.

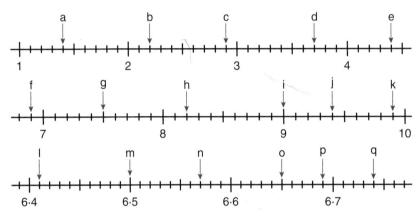

3.4 Ordering numbers with one decimal place

To compare numbers, use a number line.

Example 1
Which is bigger 4·7 or 4·3?

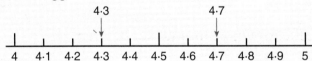

4·7 is bigger.

Example 2
Order these numbers, smallest first.

4·7, 4·1, 5·2, 4·5, 4·9, 5

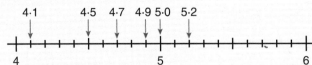

The correct order is **4·1, 4·5, 4·7, 4·9, 5, 5·2.**

> 5 is the same as 5·0.

Exercise 3.4

1 For each pair, which number is bigger:

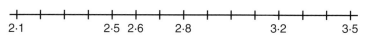

(**a**) 2·5 or 3·5   (**b**) 2·1 or 2·8   (**c**) 2·8 or 2·6
(**d**) 3·5 or 2·6   (**e**) 2·1 or 2·5   (**f**) 3·5 or 3·2
(**g**) 2·8 or 2·5   (**h**) 2·6 or 2·1   (**i**) 3·2 or 2·5?

2 For each pair, which number is bigger:
(**a**) 5·6 or 5·3   (**b**) 2·7 or 2·9   (**c**) 3·1 or 2·4
(**d**) 7·8 or 8·0   (**e**) 3·5 or 2·9   (**f**) 6·3 or 6·6?

W You need Worksheet **3.8** for question **3**.

4 Order these numbers, smallest first.
(**a**) 8·6, 8·2, 7·8, 9·1, 8·9, 7·5, 8·0, 9·3
(**b**) 17·4, 17·9, 16·9, 17·8, 16·7, 17·0, 17·5
(**c**) 3·7, 4·2, 3·5, 4·7, 3·2, 3·0, 4·5
(**d**) 2·7, 2·9, 1·7, 3·1, 2·0, 1·9, 2·3, 3·3
(**e**) 0·7, 1·5, 0·3, 1·0, 0·6, 1·2, 0·4, 0·9, 1·1

3.5 Ordering numbers with two decimal places

To compare numbers, use a number line.

Example 1
Which is bigger 6·4 or 6·31?

6·4 is the same as 6·40.

6·4 is bigger than 6·31.

Example 2
Order these numbers, smallest first.
4·17, 4·32, 4·4, 4.09, 4·25

4·4 is the same as 4·40.

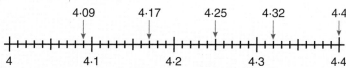

The correct order is **4·09, 4·17, 4·25, 4·32, 4·4.**

Exercise 3.5

1 For each pair, which number is bigger:

(**a**) £1.52 or £1.40   (**b**) £3.46 or £3.47   (**c**) £2.60 or £2.59

(**d**) £5.03 or £5.10   (**e**) £7.20 or £7.09   (**f**) £6.27 or £6.30?

2 For each pair, which number is bigger:

(**a**) 1·52 or 1·40   (**b**) 3·46 or 3·47   (**c**) 2·60 or 2·59

(**d**) 5·03 or 5·10   (**e**) 7·20 or 7·09   (**f**) 6·27 or 6·30?

3 For each pair, which number is bigger:

```
 +---+---+---+---+---+---+---+---+---+---+---+---+---+
 4  4·1 4·2 4·3 4·4 4·5 4·6 4·7 4·8 4·9 5·0 5·1 5·2 5·3
```

(**a**) 4·6 or 4·7   (**b**) 4·82 or 4·83   (**c**) 5·21 or 5·12

(**d**) 4·2 or 4·09   (**e**) 4·3 or 4·34   (**f**) 4·6 or 4·21

(**g**) 4·5 or 4·48   (**h**) 4·3 or 5·1   (**i**) 4·35 or 4·85

(**j**) 4·44 or 4·45   (**k**) 4 or 4·1   (**l**) 4·02 or 4·1?

4 For each pair, which number is bigger:

(**a**) 11·4 or 11·5   (**b**) 16·35 or 16·32   (**c**) 18·71 or 18·62

(**d**) 15·5 or 15·29   (**e**) 30·1 or 30·31   (**f**) 27·8 or 27·12?

5 Order these amounts of money, from smallest to largest.

(**a**) £1.54, £1.08, £1.10, £1.64, £1.31, £1.90, £1.09

(**b**) £3.06, £3.54, £3.15, £3.20, £3.72, £3.14

(**c**) £12.50, £11.60, £12.14, £11.48, £12.32, £11.70, £12.02

(**d**) £20.40, £20.14, £20.07, £20.25, £20.09, £20.18, £20.10

W You need Worksheet **3.9** for question **6**.

7 Order each list of numbers, smallest first.

(**a**) 3·74, 3·61, 3·5, 3·59, 3·67, 3·6

(**b**) 4·27, 5·84, 4·07, 5·1, 4·36, 5·7, 4·6

(**c**) 7·11, 7·45, 7·36, 7·69, 7·8, 7·14

(**d**) 5·3, 5·46, 5·03, 5·1, 5·31, 5·18

(**e**) 9·4, 10·32, 10·06, 9·78, 9·14, 10·1, 10·77

3.6 Rounding to the nearest whole number

Example

Round 16·8 to the nearest whole number.

16·8

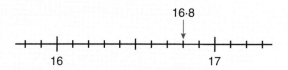

16
17

16·8 is **17** to the nearest whole number.

| 16·8 is between 16 and 17. |

| 16·8 is closer to 17 than 16. |

Exercise 3.6

W You need Worksheet **3.10** for question **1**.

2 Round each of the following to the nearest whole number.

(**a**) 6·7   (**b**) 4·3   (**c**) 1·8   (**d**) 8·1   (**e**) 12·5   (**f**) 10·9

(**g**) 27·4   (**h**) 11·1   (**i**) 0·8   (**j**) 13·6   (**k**) 8·7   (**l**) 23·2

3 Round the amount of each element to the nearest whole number.

Elements on the moon	Amount per 100 kg
Silicon	19·2
Iron	14·3
Titanium	5·9
Aluminium	5·6
Magnesium	4·5

3.7 Estimating

Example

I need 3 pieces of wood of these lengths.
Roughly how much wood will I need to buy?

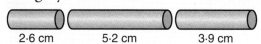

2·6 cm   5·2 cm   3·9 cm

2·6 rounds to   3
5·2 rounds to   5
3·9 rounds to   4
       Total   12

The total length is approximately **12 cm**. This is called an **estimate**.

Exercise 3.7

1 Round each length to the nearest whole number and estimate the total length.

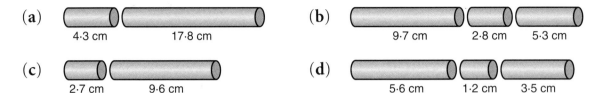

(a) 4·3 cm 17·8 cm

(b) 9·7 cm 2·8 cm 5·3 cm

(c) 2·7 cm 9·6 cm

(d) 5·6 cm 1·2 cm 3·5 cm

2 Mrs Peterson sent two parcels.
They weighed 6·8 kg and 12·4 kg.
Estimate the total weight of the two parcels.

3 Samira had a piece of ribbon 5·8 metres long.
She cut off a piece 3·3 metres long.
Estimate how much she had left.

3.8 Rounding to one decimal place

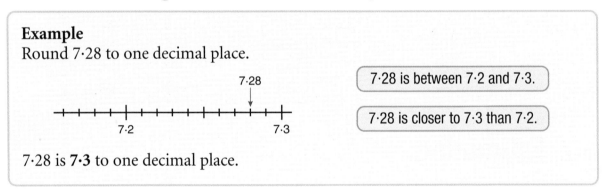

Example
Round 7·28 to one decimal place.

7·28

7·2   7·3

7·28 is between 7·2 and 7·3.

7·28 is closer to 7·3 than 7·2.

7·28 is **7·3** to one decimal place.

Exercise 3.8

W You need Worksheet **3.11** for question **1**.

2 Round each of the following to one decimal place.

(a) 6·42	(b) 3·82	(c) 5·76	(d) 1·39
(e) 5·75	(f) 8·17	(g) 12·34	(h) 21·51
(i) 16·93	(j) 4·28	(k) 11·02	(l) 18·07
(m) 9·92	(n) 9·96	(o) 10·08	(p) 15·36

3 Round these speeds to one decimal place.

Average speed of Tour de France winners		
Year	Cyclist	Speed km/h
1995	Miguel Indurain	39·19
1996	Bjarne Rijs	39·22
1997	Jan Ullrich	39·24
1998	Marco Pantani	39·98
1999	Lance Armstrong	40·28
2000	Lance Armstrong	39·57
2001	Lance Armstrong	40·07
2002	Lance Armstrong	39·92
2003	Lance Armstrong	41·02

4 Round these weights to one decimal place.

Food	Average consumed in one week (kg)
Bread	0·77
Cakes	0·33
Fruit	0·75
Milk and cream	2·01
Meat	1·03
Vegetables	0·73

5 Round each amount to one decimal place.

Region	Number per 100 who speak Gaelic
Aberdeenshire	0·39
Aberdeen	0·67
Dundee	0·45
East Ayrshire	0·31
Edinburgh	0·70
Eilean Siar	59·78
Highland	6·09
Orkney	0·48
Perth and Kinross	1·08

6 Round each amount to one decimal place.

	Average number of hours worked per week	
Region	Male	Female
Highland	44·97	31·63
Argyll and Bute	45·39	32·28
Clackmannanshire	42·60	31·58
Falkirk	42·73	31·78
Edinburgh	41·58	33·63
Glasgow	41·55	33·52
Inverclyde	41·84	31·92
Fife	42·64	31·74
Borders	43·64	31·15
Eilean Siar	44·62	30·34

3.9 Mental methods

Example

(**a**) 3·6 + 2·7

(**b**) 4·2 − 1·5

3·6 + 2·7 = **6·3**

4·2 − 1·5 = **2·7**

Exercise 3.9

1 Find the missing numbers:

(**a**) 0·2 + ☐ = 0·7   (**b**) 0·3 + 0·5 = ☐   (**c**) 0·7 + ☐ = 0·8

(**d**) 0·7 + ☐ = 0·9   (**e**) 0·6 + ☐ = 0·9   (**f**) ☐ + 0·1 = 0·2

(**g**) ☐ + 0·2 = 1·0   (**h**) 0·5 + ☐ = 1·0   (**i**) 0·4 + 0·6 = ☐

2 Find:

(**a**) 1·6 + 1·3   (**b**) 2·5 + 1·3   (**c**) 3·4 + 5·1

(**d**) 7·2 + 2·7   (**e**) 3·8 + 3·1   (**f**) 1·5 + 1·4

(**g**) 7·6 + 1·2   (**h**) 1·5 + 1·4   (**i**) 1·5 + 1·5

3 Find:

(**a**) 0·9 − 0·7 = ☐   (**b**) 0·3 − ☐ = 0·1   (**c**) 0·9 − 0·5 = ☐

(**d**) 0·6 − ☐ = 0·2   (**e**) 1·0 − ☐ = 0·7   (**f**) ☐ − 0·4 = 0·7

(**g**) 1·0 − ☐ = 0·9   (**h**) 0·8 − 0·3 = ☐   (**i**) ☐ − 0·5 = 0·1

4 Find:

(**a**) 2·9 − 1·4   (**b**) 1·8 − 0·2   (**c**) 1·6 − 0·4

(**d**) 4·8 − 2·3   (**e**) 3·7 − 2·7   (**f**) 2·9 − 2·1

(**g**) 3·9 − 2·5   (**h**) 4·7 − 2·6   (**i**) 3·2 − 3·2

5 Find:

(**a**) 2·6 + 0·5   (**b**) 2·4 − 0·7   (**c**) 1·5 − 0·7

(**d**) 1·6 + 0·6   (**e**) 2·1 − 0·9   (**f**) 5·4 + 0·8

(**g**) 2·3 − 0·4   (**h**) 2·4 + 0·7   (**i**) 1·1 − 0·6

(**j**) 0·3 + 0·9   (**k**) 3·2 − 0·5   (**l**) 1·2 + 0·8

6 James needs 1·2 kilogrammes of flour to make biscuits.
He only has 0·5 kilogrammes.
How much more flour does he need?

7 Angela's sunflower measures 0·9 metres.
In two weeks it grows another 0·3 metres.
How tall is it now?

8 When Emily was born she weighed 4·7 kilogrammes.
After one week she had gained 0·5 kilogrammes.
How much did she then weigh?

9 Mr Costello checks the temperature every hour.
At 3 p.m. the temperature was 5·7 °C and at 4 p.m. the temperature was 6·5 °C.
By how much had the temperature risen?

3.10 Adding and subtracting

Example 1

Ellie buys a card costing £2·65 and
wrapping paper costing 85 pence.

```
    2·65
  + 0·85
    3·50
    1  1
```

The total cost is **£3.50.**

Example 2

Andy has a piece of pipe 35 centimetres
long. If he cuts off a piece 19·2 centimetres
long, how much pipe will be left?

```
      2 1 4
    3 5·0
  −  19·2
    15·8
```

15·8 cm will be left.

Exercise 3.10

 You need Worksheet **3.12** for questions **1** and **2**.

3 Charlie weighed 85·3 kilogrammes.
After dieting he weighed 74·5 kilogrammes.
How much weight had he lost?

4 Mrs Morgan posts three parcels.
The postage for the parcels is £3.45,
£1.82 and 75 pence.
What was the total cost?

5 Graeme buys newspapers and magazines costing £2.99, £2.65 and 85 pence. How much will this cost in total?

6 Abbas has £35. He buys his lunch, which costs £8.86. How much does he have left?

7 Mr Brown has a piece of wood 3 metres long. If he cuts off a piece 1·54 metres long, how much wood will be left?

8 Gemma is working in a laboratory. She takes notes in her workbook.

	Start of experiment	End of experiment
Temperature (°C)	8·5	15·7

By how much did the temperature rise?

9 When Abbey was six her height was 78·4 centimetres. When she was twenty-six her height was 163·5 centimetres. By how much had she grown?

10 A small boat can carry up to 250 kilogrammes of cargo.

75·5 kg A   48·2 kg B   80·9 kg C   132·5 kg D   100·1 kg E

Find 3 ways of loading the boat with at least two boxes and calculate the total weight each time.

11 A lift can carry 300 kilogrammes. Four people get on the lift. Their weights are 82·4 kg, 65·3 kg, 42·9 kg and 82·7 kg.

(**a**) Find the total weight of these people.

(**b**) How much more weight can the lift safely carry?

(**c**) Jill weighs 63·8 kilogrammes.
Can Jill join the others on the lift safely?
Give a reason for your answer.

W You need Worksheet **3.13** for question **12**.

3.11 Multiplying

Example   Tatsumi buys seven cushions costing £8.65 each.
What is the total cost?

$$
\begin{array}{r}
8{\cdot}65 \\
\times\quad 7 \\
\hline
60{\cdot}55 \\
\small{4\ 3} \\
\end{array}
$$

Total cost is **£60.55**.

Exercise 3.11

You need Worksheet **3.14** for question **1**.

2 A farm charges £3.40 per kilogramme for strawberries.
Mrs Frost buys 8 kilogrammes. How much will this cost?

3 Evelyn needs 5 pieces of ribbon, each 2·4 metres long.
How much ribbon will she need altogether?

4 (**a**) Angela buys seven 1·5 litre bottles of water.
How much water is this?
(**b**) If each bottle costs £1.09, what is the total cost?

5 (**a**) Find the cost for 6 copies of the magazine
at normal price.
(**b**) How much money is saved with
the special offer?

> **SPECIAL OFFER!**
> **6** issues
> for **£15**
> normal price £2.65
> per issue

6 Kate buys 9 DVDs costing £8.95 each.
How much did she pay in total?

7 Miss Munro bought 3 jigsaws costing £2.99 each and
4 puzzles costing £1.75 each.
(**a**) Find the total cost of the jigsaws.
(**b**) Find the total cost of the puzzles.
(**c**) Find the total amount Miss Munro spent.

8 (**a**) Find Anna's change from £5 if she buys 3 scones.
(**b**) Mr Williamson buys 4 rolls and a pasty.
How much change will he receive from £2?
(**c**) Find Mrs Dobson's change from £10 if
she buys a sponge cake and 5 pancakes.

> **Walker's Bakery**
>
> | | |
> |---|---|
> | scones | 46p each |
> | pancakes | 32p each |
> | loaves | 85p each |
> | rolls | 24p each |
> | pasties | 76p each |
> | sponge cake | £1.80 |
> | fruit loaf | £1.65 |

3.12 Dividing

Example 1

Deepa has 34·2 metres of rope to be cut into six equal pieces.
How long is each piece?

$$\begin{array}{r} 5.\,7 \\ 6)\overline{34.^42} \end{array}$$

Each piece is **5·7 metres** long.

Example 2

Mr Robertson shares £142 equally among his five grandchildren.
How much does each receive?

$$\begin{array}{r} 2\,8.\,4 \\ 5)\overline{14^42.^20} \end{array}$$

> Instead of leaving a remainder add zeros after the decimal point.

Each grandchild receives **£28.40.**

> Amounts of money must have two decimal places.

Exercise 3.12

W You need Worksheet **3.15** for questions **1** and **2**.

3 If 28·2 kilogrammes of nails are split equally into six small boxes, what weight of nails will be in each box?

4 Alice paid £3.60 for 9 roses. How much did one rose cost?

5 Mr Sanderson's prize-winning 76·4 kilogramme cabbage is shared equally among 4 people.
How much did each person receive?

6 Seven kilogrammes of sweets are shared equally among 5 buckets.
What weight of sweets will be in each bucket?

7 A lottery win of £162 was shared equally among 8 people.
How much did each receive?

8 Twenty-six metres of rope is split into 8 equal pieces.
How long is each piece?

3.13 Multiplying by 10 and 100

To multiply a number by 10, you move every digit one place to the left.

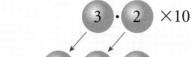

gives

which is written as 32.

To multiply a number by 100, you move every digit two places to the left.

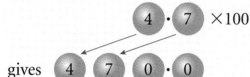

gives

which is written as 470.

Example

(**a**) $5·6 \times 10 = $ **56**
(**b**) $1·34 \times 10 = $ **13·4**
(**c**) $1·7 \times 100 = $ **170**
(**b**) $3·08 \times 100 = $ **308**

Exercise 3.13

1 Find:
   (**a**) $4·1 \times 10$ (**b**) $3·2 \times 10$ (**c**) $6·8 \times 10$
   (**d**) $37·2 \times 10$ (**e**) $8·6 \times 10$ (**f**) $0·4 \times 10$

2 Find:
   (**a**) $1·91 \times 10$ (**b**) $5·46 \times 10$ (**c**) $8·07 \times 10$
   (**d**) $0·53 \times 10$ (**e**) $0·67 \times 10$ (**f**) $51·38 \times 10$

3 Find:
   (**a**) $2·7 \times 10$ (**b**) $3·12 \times 10$ (**c**) $0·56 \times 10$
   (**d**) $1·78 \times 10$ (**e**) $15·64 \times 10$ (**f**) $19·08 \times 10$
   (**g**) $12·03 \times 10$ (**h**) $1·3 \times 10$ (**i**) $0·7 \times 10$

4 Find:
   (**a**) $8·2 \times 100$ (**b**) $1·7 \times 100$ (**c**) $4·2 \times 100$
   (**d**) $3·7 \times 100$ (**e**) $2·6 \times 100$ (**f**) $5·9 \times 100$
   (**g**) $20·5 \times 100$ (**h**) $0·3 \times 100$ (**i**) $0·6 \times 100$

5 Find:
  (**a**) 17·17 × 100   (**b**) 13·64 × 100   (**c**) 38·05 × 100
  (**d**) 22·75 × 100   (**e**) 6·47 × 100   (**f**) 8·01 × 100
  (**g**) 10·2 × 100   (**h**) 0·45 × 100   (**i**) 0·22 × 100

6 Find:
  (**a**) 45·2 × 10   (**b**) 23·6 × 10   (**c**) 50·6 × 100
  (**d**) 25·8 × 10   (**e**) 6·3 × 100   (**f**) 5·7 × 10
  (**g**) 62·5 × 100   (**h**) 36·5 × 10   (**i**) 0·92 × 100
  (**j**) 1·41 × 100   (**k**) 7·09 × 100   (**l**) 83·05 × 10

7 A picture hook weighs 0·7 grammes. Calculate the weight of:
  (**a**) 10 hooks   (**b**) 100 hooks.

8 Alice can buy a biro pen for £0.14 at her local shop.
  At the 'Cash and Carry' she can buy 100 pens for £12.65.
  (**a**) Calculate the cost of buying 100 pens at the local shop.
  (**b**) Which is best value for money? Give a reason for your answer.

9 Council tax is paid in 10 monthly instalments.
  (**a**) Mel pays £87.38 each month. How much will she pay in total?
  (**b**) Rudi pays £106.20 each month. How much will he pay in total?

3.14 Dividing by 10 and 100

To divide a number by 10, you move every digit one place to the right.

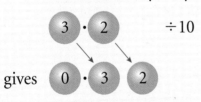

To divide a number by 100, you move every digit two places to the right.

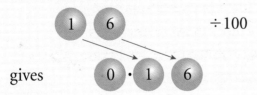

Example
(**a**) 98 ÷ 10 = **9·8**   (**b**) 201 ÷ 10 = **20·1**
(**c**) 740 ÷ 100 = **7·4**   (**b**) 6 ÷ 100 = **0·06**

Exercise 3.14

1 Find:

   (**a**) 47 ÷ 10   (**b**) 63 ÷ 10   (**c**) 88 ÷ 10

   (**d**) 390 ÷ 10   (**e**) 164 ÷ 10   (**f**) 870 ÷ 10

2 Find:

   (**a**) 7·2 ÷ 10   (**b**) 9·4 ÷ 10   (**c**) 1·3 ÷ 10

   (**d**) 0·5 ÷ 10   (**e**) 40·6 ÷ 10   (**f**) 36·8 ÷ 10

3 Find:

   (**a**) 0·7 ÷ 10   (**b**) 1·4 ÷ 10   (**c**) 15·9 ÷ 10

   (**d**) 27·9 ÷ 10   (**e**) 66·7 ÷ 10   (**f**) 90·1 ÷ 10

4 Find:

   (**a**) 116 ÷ 100   (**b**) 238 ÷ 100   (**c**) 579 ÷ 100

   (**d**) 85 ÷ 100   (**e**) 15 ÷ 100   (**f**) 60 ÷ 100

   (**g**) 78 ÷ 100   (**h**) 356 ÷ 100   (**i**) 50 ÷ 100

   (**j**) 3 ÷ 100   (**k**) 4 ÷ 100   (**l**) 6 ÷ 100

5 Find:

   (**a**) 65 ÷ 10   (**b**) 4056 ÷ 10   (**c**) 8100 ÷ 100

   (**d**) 200 ÷ 100   (**e**) 28·6 ÷ 10   (**f**) 43 ÷ 10

   (**g**) 405 ÷ 10   (**h**) 165 ÷ 100   (**i**) 18·4 ÷ 10

6 A packet of 10 sweets weighs 52 grammes.
   Find the weight of one sweet.

7 A packet of 100 sharpeners weighs 632 grammes.
   Find the weight of one sharpener.

8 Council tax is paid in 10 monthly instalments.

   (**a**) Margaret's council tax bill is £870. How much is each instalment?

   (**b**) Rahman's council tax bill is £1037. How much is each instalment?

   (**c**) Mr Malcolm's council tax bill is £1240. How much is each instalment?

9 Find:

   (**a**) 6·5 × 10   (**b**) 413·4 ÷ 10   (**c**) 51·74 × 100

   (**d**) 250 ÷ 100   (**e**) 28·6 × 10   (**f**) 4·6 ÷ 100

   (**g**) 0·5 ÷ 10   (**h**) 37 ÷ 100   (**i**) 5·6 × 100

   (**j**) 8 ÷ 100   (**k**) 80 ÷ 100   (**l**) 0·9 ÷ 10

3.15 Using a calculator

£7 − £5.60  **Answer £1.40**

£6 − £4.95 | 6 − 4.95 | | = | | 1.05 | **Answer £1.05**

Example
Calculate the cost of 12 pens at 87 pence each.

> When using a calculator with money calculations the answer 1·05 means £1.05 and 1·5 means £1.50.

| 0.87 × 12 | | = | | 10.44 | The cost is **£10.44**

Exercise 3.15

1 Calculate:
  (**a**) £104 + £21.30   (**b**) £1650 − £297.60
  (**c**) £6995 − £299.50   (**d**) £107.60 − £54.56
  (**e**) £2076.70 − £395.40   (**f**) £2000 − £560.70
  (**g**) £4056.90 + £123.40   (**h**) £4355.89 + £2451.56

2 Calculate the cost of:
  (**a**) 34 lollipops at 16 pence each
  (**b**) 70 pens at 15 pence each
  (**c**) 45 notepads at 32 pence each
  (**d**) 26 apples at 20 pence each
  (**e**) 40 candles at 42 pence each.

W You need Worksheet **3.16** for questions **3** and **4**.

5 Lena has a lottery win of £9 648 227.53.
If she invests £7 565 000, how much will she have left?

6 Calculate:
  (**a**) 14·325 − 6·74   (**b**) 64·83 + 204·77   (**c**) 1610 − 3·72
  (**d**) 132·3 − 117·17   (**e**) 16·4 × 18   (**f**) 73·4 × 35
  (**g**) 14·04 × 23   (**h**) 45·67 × 13   (**i**) 37·06 × 25

7 A man pays for his new car in 24 instalments of £315.50.
How much did he pay in total?

8 Graeme pays 40 pence each time he crosses the Mulbray Road Bridge.
If he crosses the bridge twice each day, how much will he
have paid after six weeks?

9 Car parking on Princess Square costs 40 pence for 15 minutes.
How much would it cost someone to park for:
(**a**) 30 minutes   (**b**) 1 hour   (**c**) 6 hours?

10 Find:
(**a**) 3·12 × 20   (**b**) 20·4 ÷ 30   (**c**) 263·4 × 900
(**d**) 150·6 ÷ 300   (**e**) 31·4 × 50   (**f**) 5·2 ÷ 200
(**g**) 91 ÷ 700   (**h**) 3·7 × 300   (**i**) 20 ÷ 500

3.16 Making sense of answers

Freya needs 34 tiles to tile
her bathroom.
Tiles are sold in packs of 8.
How many packs will she need?

34 ÷ 8 = 4·25

4 packs contain 32.
5 packs contain 40.
Freya needs more than 4 packs so
she will need to buy **5 packs** and
there will be 6 left over.

14 chocolates are to be shared equally
among 4 people.
How many chocolates will each person
receive?

14 ÷ 4 = 3·5

There are not enough for four each so
each person will receive **3 chocolates**
and there will be 2 left over.

Exercise 3.16

1 David needs 68 tiles for his kitchen. If the tiles are sold
in packs of 5, how many packs will he need to buy?

2 Andreas wants to buy 200 balloons for a school dance.
If balloons are sold in packs of 15, how many packs
will he have to buy?

3 A school trip is being run for 270 pupils.
If a bus holds 46 people, how many buses will be needed for the trip?

4 Annie, Arnie and Alex are sharing marbles equally among themselves.
   (**a**) If there are 85 marbles, how many will they each receive?
   (**b**) How many will be left over?

5 Julie can buy a wooden puzzle for £6.
   (**a**) How many will she be able to buy if she has £50?
   (**b**) How much money will she have left?

6 Arnold is packing apples into boxes holding 40 apples.
If he has 1254 apples, how many boxes will he need?

7 The lift in the Dungow Science Centre holds 8 people.
If a group of 63 people are waiting to go to the top of the
tower, how many trips in the lift will this take?

8 Rhys calculates that he can save £30 each week.
He needs to pay for a holiday costing £315.
How many weeks will he need to save?

9 Mrs Baxter is knitting jackets for her baby granddaughter.
She knows that each jacket will use three balls of wool.
   (**a**) If she has 20 balls of wool, how may jackets will she be
        able to knit?
   (**b**) How many balls of wool will be left?

Review exercise 3

   1 Write the number represented by the shading in each picture.

   (**a**)

   (**b**)

   2 Write the number represented by the shading in each picture.

   (**a**)

   (**b**)
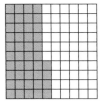

3 Write the value of each letter.

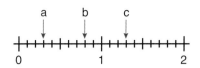 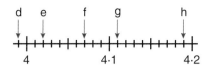

4 Order these numbers, smallest first.

(**a**) 5·1, 5·4, 4·8, 6·1, 4·9, 5·5, 4·0, 3·8

(**b**) 10·4, 11·1, 11·9, 12·8, 11·7, 10·0, 11·2

(**c**) 2·1, 3·45, 2·36, 2·69, 3·8, 2·14

(**d**) 15·2, 15·47, 15·04, 15·1, 15·31, 15·48

5 Round each of the following to the nearest whole number.

(**a**) 3·4   (**b**) 2·8   (**c**) 10·7   (**d**) 12·2

6 Round each of the following to one decimal place.

(**a**) 5·36   (**b**)1·83   (**c**) 13·98   (**d**) 25·45

7 Copy and complete:

(**a**)   1·7   (**b**)   1·2   (**c**)   5·4   (**d**)   3·1
      + 0·8   + 0·7   + 0·6   + 0·5
      _____   _____   _____   _____

8 Copy and complete:

(**a**)   4·36   (**b**) 4)61·6   (**c**)   17·09   (**d**) 4)138
       ×   3   ×   6
       _____   _____

9 Find:

(**a**) 21·8 × 10   (**b**) 24·17 × 100   (**c**) 21·16 × 100

(**d**) 12·9 × 100   (**e**) 10·27 × 10   (**f**) 35·04 × 100

(**g**) 32 ÷ 10   (**h**) 3177 ÷ 10   (**i**) 76 ÷ 100

(**j**) 70 ÷ 100   (**k**) 13·5 ÷ 10   (**l**) 730 ÷ 10

10 Mrs Donaldson can buy a napkin for £4.

(**a**) How many will she be able to buy if she has £35?

(**b**) How much money will she have left?

11 Rosslyn wants to buy 40 fairy cakes for her birthday party.
If the cakes are sold in packs of 6, how many packs will she need to buy?

12 Tony buys newspapers and magazines costing £3.85, £6.99
and 72 pence. How much will this cost in total?

13 Kate buys 7 CDs costing £6.45 each.
How much does she pay in total?

14 A lottery win of £190 is shared equally among 8 people.
How much does each receive?

 15 Copy and complete this bill.

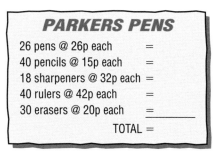

PARKERS PENS

26 pens @ 26p each	=
40 pencils @ 15p each	=
18 sharpeners @ 32p each	=
40 rulers @ 42p each	=
30 erasers @ 20p each	= _____
TOTAL	=

Summary

Tenths and hundredths

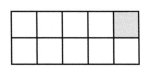

- In each of these shapes $\frac{1}{10}$ is shaded.

  As a decimal fraction, this is written 0·1

  > 0·1 is the same as $\frac{1}{10}$.

- In this shape $\frac{3}{10}$ is shaded.

  As a decimal fraction, this is written 0·3

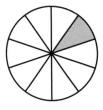

> 0·3 is the same as $\frac{3}{10}$.

$\frac{1}{100}$ written as a decimal fraction is 0·01

Place value

H	T	U	·	Tths	Hths	
		7	·	6		This number has one decimal place.
		3	·	2	5	This number has two decimal places.
1	4		·	3	0	This number has two decimal places.

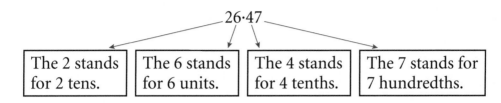

| The 2 stands for 2 tens. | The 6 stands for 6 units. | The 4 stands for 4 tenths. | The 7 stands for 7 hundredths. |

Rounding numbers

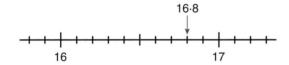

16·8 is between 16 and 17.
16·8 is closer to 17 than 16.

16·8 is 17 to the nearest whole number.

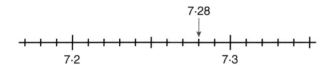

7·28 is between 7·2 and 7·3.
7·28 is closer to 7·3 than 7·2.

7·28 is 7·3 to one decimal place.

4 Angles

In this chapter you will learn to work with and extend your knowledge of angles.

4.1 Turning

Remember
An angle is an amount of turn.

 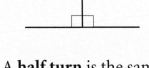 

A **quarter turn** is called a **right angle**. One right angle is 90°.

A **half turn** is the same as 2 right angles. Two right angles added together make a **straight angle**. A straight angle is 180°.

A **complete turn** is the same as 4 right angles. A complete turn is 360°.

Right angles and straight angles may be seen in everyday objects.

The red angle is a right angle. The blue angle is a straight angle.

Exercise 4.1

 You need Worksheet **4.1** for question **1**.

2 Look at the picture of this room. List where you can see a:

(**a**) right angle

(**b**) straight angle.

3 Look around the classroom.

(**a**) Make a list of objects that contain right angles.

(**b**) Make a list of objects that contain a straight angle.

4.2 Naming angles

An angle is formed where two **arms** meet at a **vertex**.

arm

vertex

arm

Look at this diagram.

The arms are PT and TX.

The vertex is at T.

The angle is called ∠PTX.

∠ means angle.

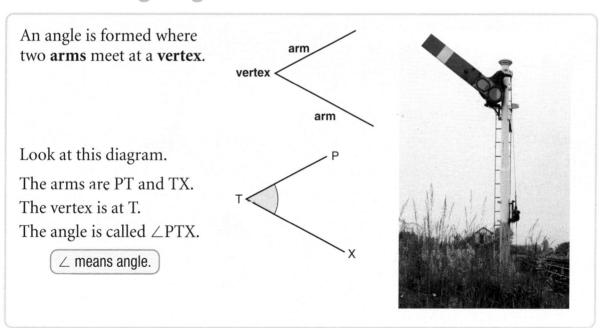

Exercise 4.2

W You need Worksheet **4.2** for question **1**.

2 Name each shaded angle.

(**a**)
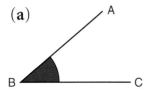

(**b**)
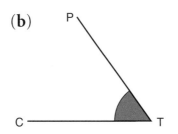

(**c**)
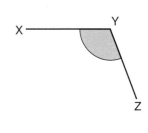

(**d**)
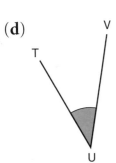

(**e**)
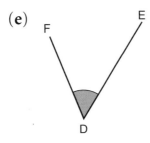

3 Name each shaded angle.

(**a**)
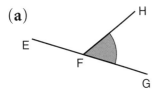

(**b**)
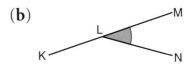

(**c**)
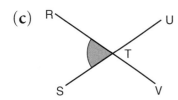

(**d**)
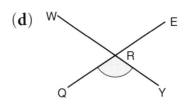

4 In triangle ABC name the angle shaded:
(**a**) red
(**b**) blue
(**c**) yellow

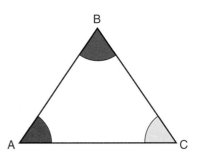

5 Copy these diagrams and shade the named angle.

(**a**) ∠CBD
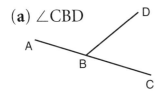

(**b**) ∠PNM
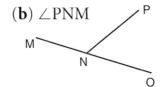

(**c**) ∠JHG
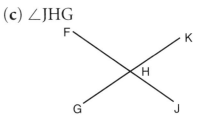

6 Name all the right angles in these diagrams.

(a)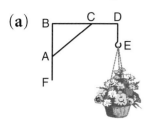

(b)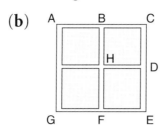

(c)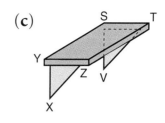

4.3 Types of angles

- An acute angle is smaller than a right angle.
  An acute angle lies between 0° and 90°.

- An obtuse angle is bigger than a right angle
  and smaller than a straight angle.
  An obtuse angle lies between 90° and 180°.

- A reflex angle is bigger than a straight angle.
  A reflex angle lies between 180° and 360°.

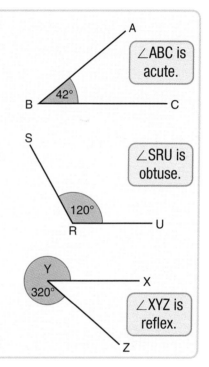

∠ABC is acute.

∠SRU is obtuse.

∠XYZ is reflex.

Exercise 4.3

W You need Worksheets **4.3** and **4.4** for questions **1** and **2**.
You need red, blue and yellow coloured pencils.

3 Name: (a) an acute angle
          (b) an obtuse angle
          (c) a straight angle.

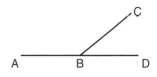

4 Copy each diagram.

(a)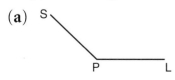

(b)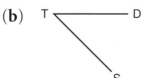

(c)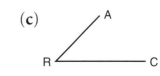

Colour: • an acute angle red • an obtuse angle blue.

5 (**a**) Draw an acute angle and name it ∠PQR.

(**b**) Draw an obtuse angle and name it ∠XYZ.

(**c**) Draw a reflex angle and name it ∠STV.

W **6** You need Worksheet **4.5**.
Cut out each card.
Make a separate pile of each type of angle.

7 You need the cards from Worksheet **4.5**.
This is a game of *Pairs* for two players.

- Shuffle the 20 cards.
- Lay them face down in 5 rows of 4.
- Player One turns over two cards.
- If the angles are the same type, keep the cards and turn over 2 more cards.
- If they do not match, replace the cards face down. It is now Player Two's turn.
- Play until all the cards have been used.
- The winner is the player with most cards.

4.4 Measuring angles

Find the size of ∠PQR.

Step 1   Place the centre of the protractor on Q with the base line on PQ as shown.

Step 2   Use the scale that has a zero on arm PQ. Count round and read the value where QR cuts the scale.

Step 3   Write the size of ∠PQR.

∠**PQR** = **125°**

There are two scales on the protractor.
Be careful to use the correct scale.

Exercise 4.4

1 Write the size of the angle in each diagram.

(**a**)

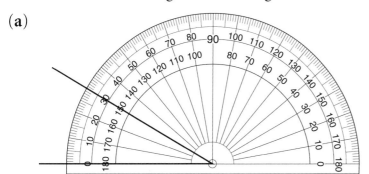

(**b**)

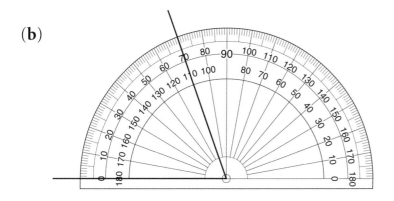

(**c**)

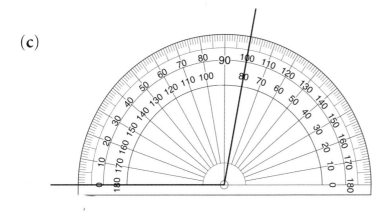

(**d**)

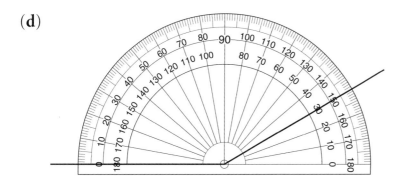

2 For each angle, write whether it is acute or obtuse and measure it.

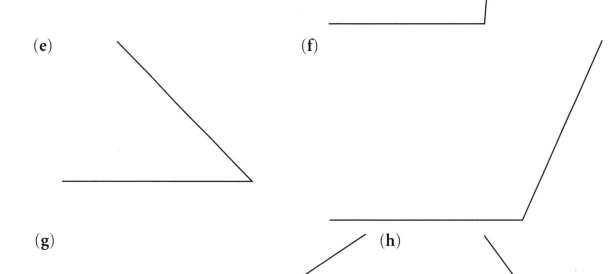

(a)

(b)

(c)

(d)

(e)

(f)

(g)

(h)

W You need Worksheet **4.6** for question **3**.

4 For each angle, write whether it is acute or obtuse and measure it.
(Sometimes it helps to turn the page and keep the protractor horizontal.)

(**a**)

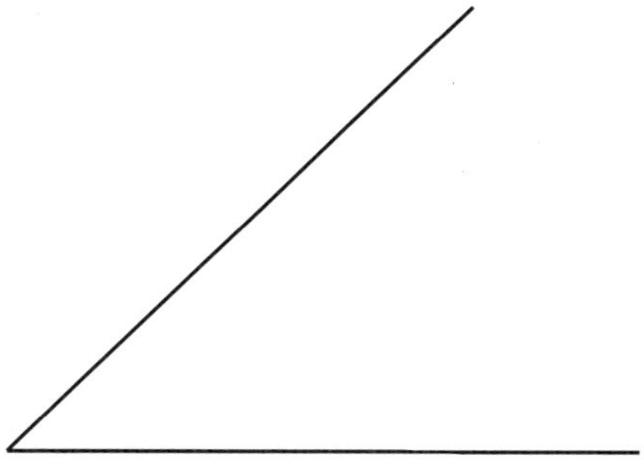

(**b**)

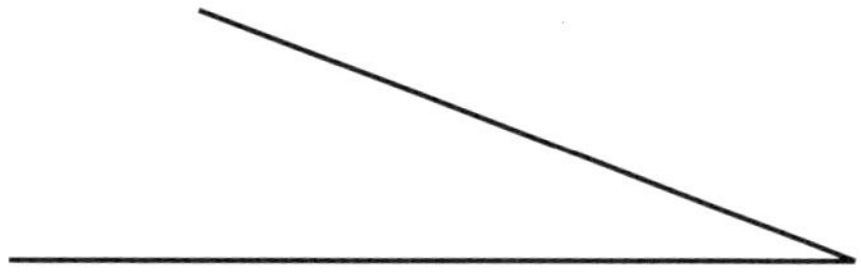

(**c**)

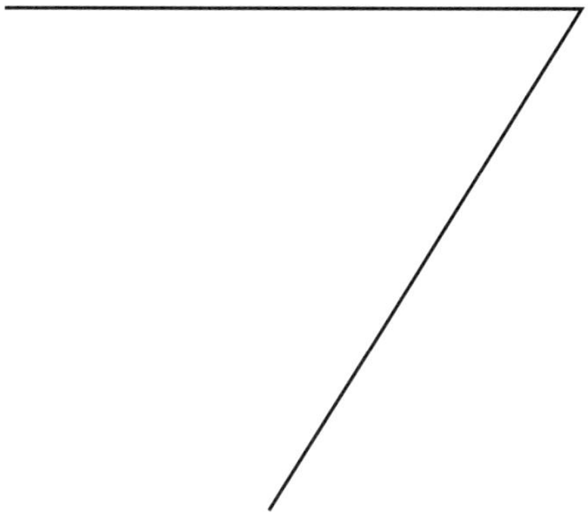

(**d**)

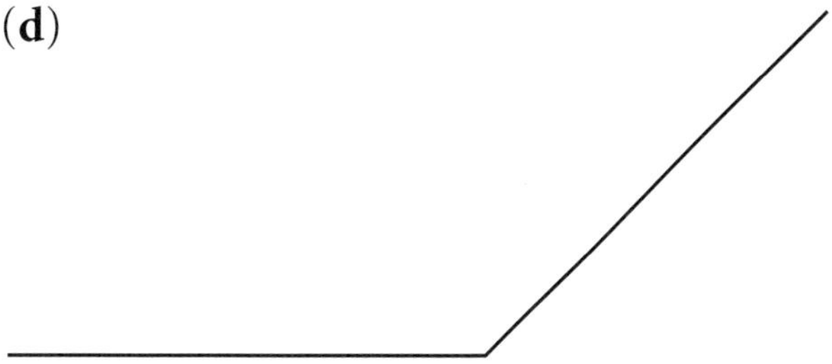

(**e**)

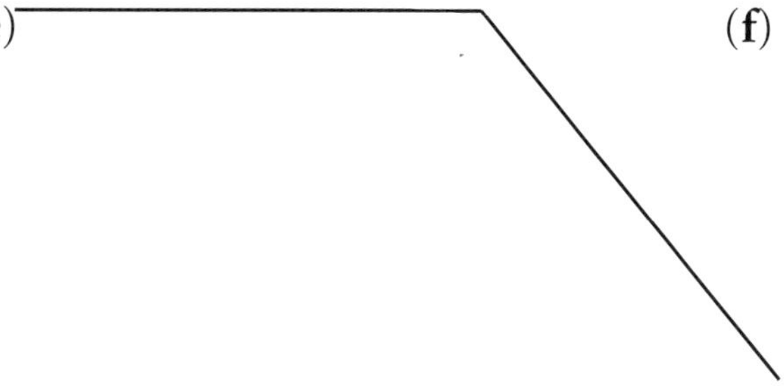

(**f**)

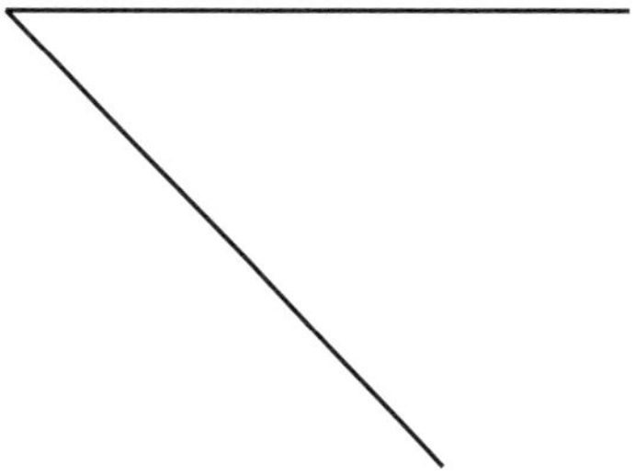

(**g**)

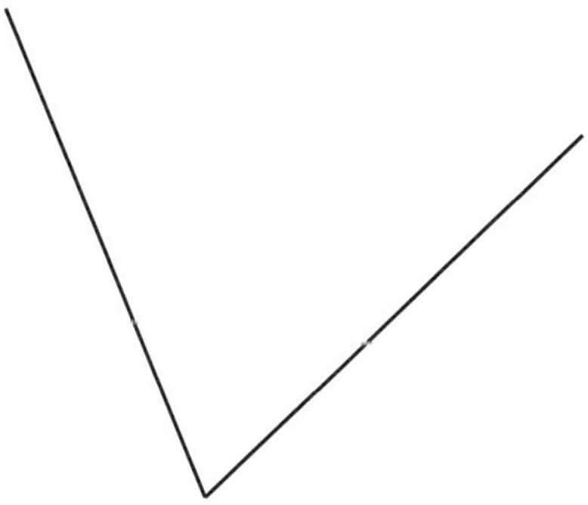

(**h**)

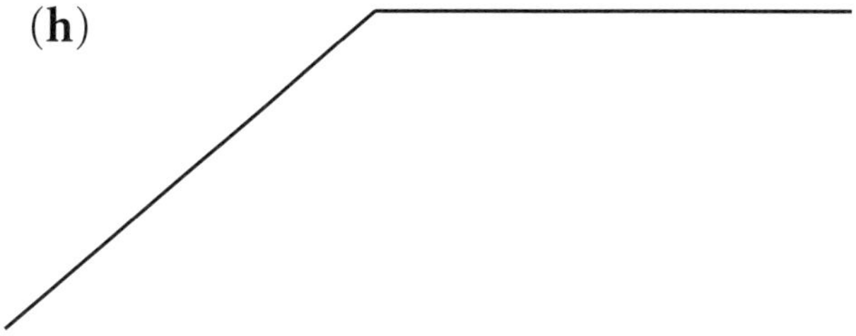

(**i**)

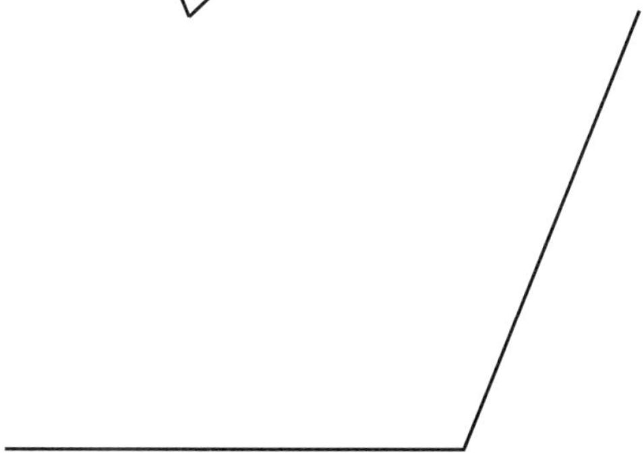

4.5 Drawing angles

Remember

Draw ∠XYZ = 53°. You need a ruler and a protractor

Step 1   Draw line XY 6 cm long.   X————————Y

Step 2   Place the centre of the protractor on Y
with the base line on XY as shown.

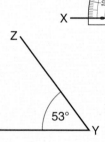

Step 3   Find the zero that is on the line XY;
count up the number of degrees and
put a dot at 53°.

Step 4   Draw a line from Y through
the dot and mark Z.

Step 5   Label your angle as shown.

Exercise 4.5

W You need Worksheet **4.7** for question **1**.

2 Draw accurately the following angles.

(**a**) ∠ABC = 50°   (**b**) ∠ABC = 30°

(**c**) ∠ABC = 85°   (**d**) ∠ABC = 75°

(**e**) ∠PQR = 45°   (**f**) ∠MNO = 17°

(**g**) ∠JKL = 34°   (**h**) ∠STU = 63°

(**i**) ∠RST = 11°

3 Draw accurately the following angles.

(**a**) ∠XYZ = 110°   (**b**) ∠DEF = 120°

(**c**) ∠GHI = 165°   (**d**) ∠PQR = 135°

(**e**) ∠MNO = 173°   (**f**) ∠JKL = 134°

4.6 Calculating with right angles

The red and the blue angles fit together to make a right angle of 90°.

Example
Calculate the size of the shaded angle.

The shaded angle is 90° − 50° = **40°**

Exercise 4.6

1 Calculate the size of the shaded angle in each diagram.

(**a**) 30°

(**b**) 40°

(**c**) 35°

2 Calculate the shaded angle in each diagram.

(**a**) 60°

(**b**) 50°

(**c**)  25°

(**d**) 24°

(**e**) 78°

(**f**) 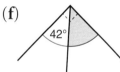 42°

4.7 Calculating with straight angles

The yellow and the green angles fit together to make a straight angle of 180°.

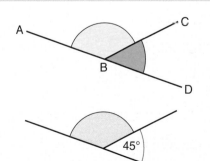

Example
Calculate the size of the shaded angle.

The shaded angle is 180° − 45° = **135°**

Exercise 4.7

1 Calculate the size of the shaded angle in each diagram.

(a)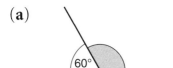

(b)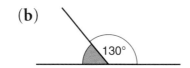

(c)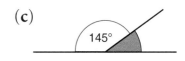

2 Calculate the shaded angle in each diagram.

(a)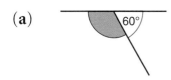

(b)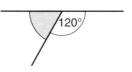

(c)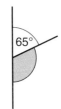

(d)

(e)

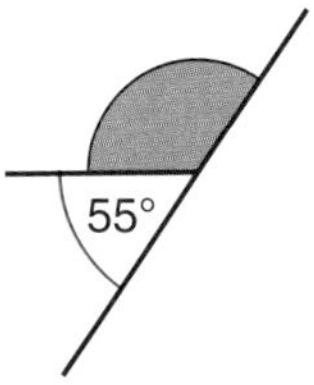

(f)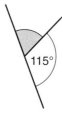

3 For each shaded angle:
- state whether it is acute or obtuse
- calculate its size.

(a)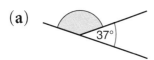

(b)

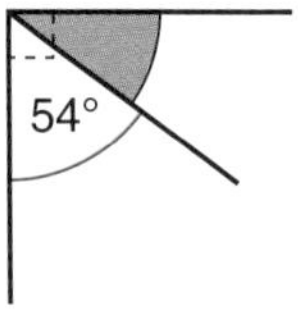

(c)

(d)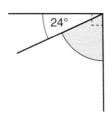

(e)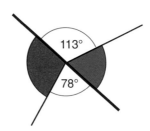

4.8 Compass points

Directions can be given using compass points.

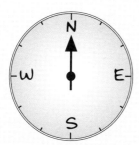

Iona has been given these directions to get from the bus station to the cinema.

- Walk north until you reach the traffic lights.
- Turn east and walk past the shop.
- Turn south and walk until you reach a garage.
- Turn east and walk until you see the cinema.

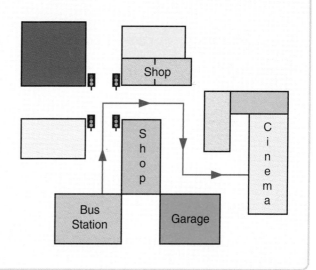

Exercise 4.8

1 Give directions for Iona to get from the cinema back to the bus station.

2 The map shows Loch Crogall. List buildings on the:

(**a**) east side

(**b**) west side

(**c**) north side

(**d**) south side.

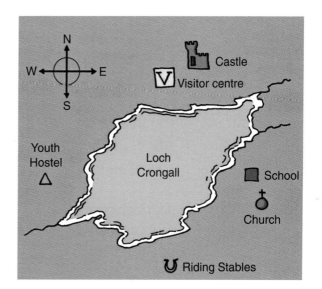

4.9 More compass points

Between the main compass points there are other directions.

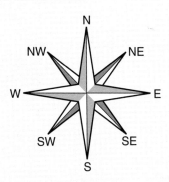

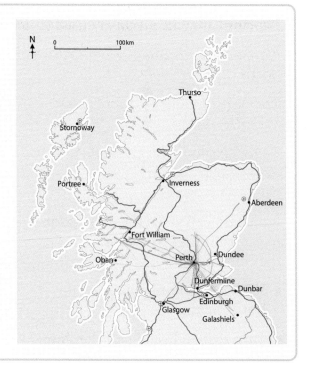

From Edinburgh, Portree is north west.

From Stornoway, Inverness is south east.

Exercise 4.9

1 From Perth, what lies to the:
   (**a**) north   (**b**) west   (**c**) south   (**d**) north west
   (**e**) south west   (**f**) north east   (**g**) south east?

2 What is the direction of Perth from:
   (**a**) Dunfermline   (**b**) Aberdeen   (**c**) Galashiels
   (**d**) Thurso   (**e**) Oban   (**f**) Portree?

3 If you fly north from Glasgow until you reach Inverness,
   then turn to the west, over what town would you next fly?

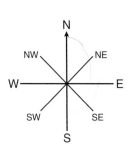

4 What is the size of the smaller angle between:
   (**a**) N and E   (**b**) S and SW   (**c**) W and N
   (**d**) NE and SW   (**e**) N and SE   (**f**) N and SW?

5 If you were facing north and turned in a clockwise direction,
   in which direction would you be facing if you turned through
   each of the following angles:
   (**a**) 90°   (**b**) 180°   (**c**) 45°   (**d**) 270°?

4.10 Three-figure bearings

Bearings are angles that are used to give directions.

Three-figure bearings are measured clockwise from north.

The bearing of north is 000°, east is 090°, south west is 225°.

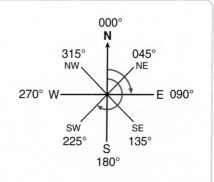

The map shows the path of a mail boat sailing across a small loch.

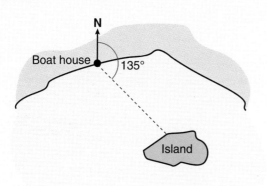

The bearing of the island from the boat house is **135°**.

Exercise 4.10

1 Write these directions as three-figure bearings.

(**a**) north   (**b**) south   (**c**) east   (**d**) west   (**e**) north east

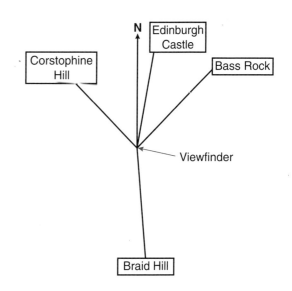

You need Worksheet **4.8** for question **2**.

3 You need a protractor.
The diagram shows a viewfinder at the top of Blackford Hill. Measure the bearing of each of the following places.

(**a**) Edinburgh Castle

(**b**) The Bass Rock

(**c**) Braid Hill

(**d**) Corstophine Hill

4 Use the map of Scotland to give the bearing of each of the following from Perth.

(**a**) Thurso

(**b**) Aberdeen

(**c**) Dunfermline

(**d**) Oban

(**e**) Portree

(**f**) Stranraer

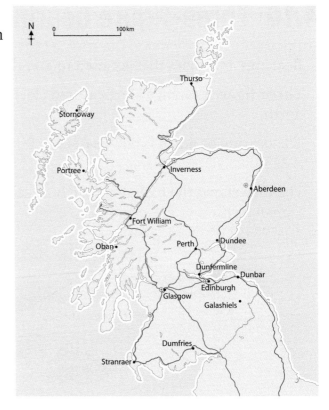

Review exercise 4

You need a protractor and red, blue and yellow coloured pencils.

1 Name the right angles in each diagram.

(**a**)

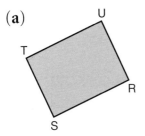

(**b**)

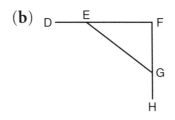

2 Copy these angles. Shade:

(**a**) the acute angle red

(**b**) the obtuse angle blue

(**c**) the reflex angle yellow.

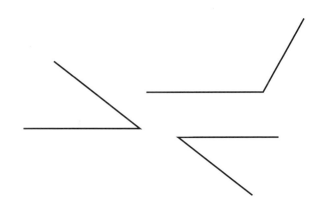

3 Measure the size of each angle.

(**a**)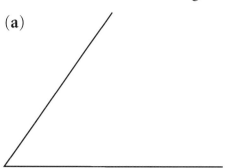

(**b**)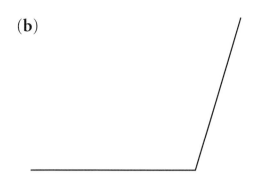

4 Draw the following angles.

(**a**) ∠ABC = 60°   (**b**) ∠HIJ = 32°   (**c**) ∠XYZ = 145°

5 For each shaded angle: • state whether it is acute or obtuse
                              • calculate its size.

(**a**) 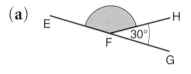   (**b**) 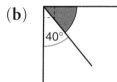   (**c**)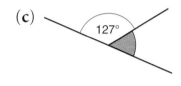

6 From the start, which buoy lies to the:

(**a**) north   (**b**) east

(**c**) south   (**d**) south west?

7 What is the direction of the finish from:

(**a**) buoy 1   (**b**) buoy 3

(**c**) buoy 4?

8 Write these directions as bearings.

(**a**) east   (**b**) north east

(**c**) south   (**d**) south west

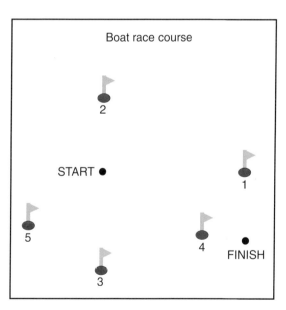

9 You need a protractor.
The diagram shows a viewfinder designed for the top of Cairngorm. Measure the bearing of each of the following places from Cairngorm.

(**a**) Bynack More

(**b**) Lochnagar

(**c**) Braeriach

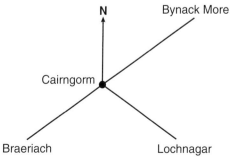

Summary

Naming angles

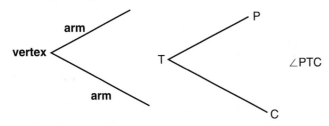

∠PTC

Types of angles

A **quarter turn** is called a **right angle**. One right angle is 90°.

A **half turn** is the same as 2 right angles. Two right angles added together make a **straight angle**. A straight angle is 180°.

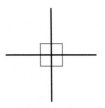

A **complete turn** is the same as 4 right angles. A complete turn is 360°.

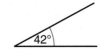

An **acute** angle lies between 0° and 90°.

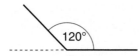

An **obtuse** angle lies between 90° and 180°.

An **reflex** angle lies between 180° and 360°.

Compass points can be used to give directions.

Bearings are angles that are used to give directions.

Three-figure bearings are measured clockwise from north.

The bearing of north is 000°, east is 090°, south west is 225°.

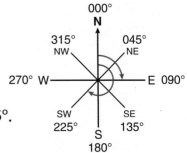

5 Fractions

In this chapter you will review your knowledge of fractions, learn about equivalent fractions and decimal equivalence.

5.1 Finding fractions

Example   Fred has 11 sweets.

$\frac{1}{11}$ of the sweets are red.

$\frac{2}{11}$ of the sweets are green.

$\frac{3}{11}$ of the sweets are blue.

$\frac{5}{11}$ of the sweets are pink.

Exercise 5.1

1 For each group, write the fraction that is red.

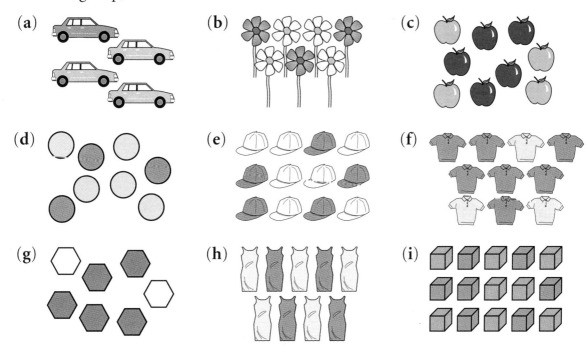

(a)
(b)
(c)
(d)
(e)
(f)
(g)
(h)
(i)

W You need Worksheet **5.1** for questions **2**, **3** and **4**.

5 Write the fraction of each shape that is red.

(a) 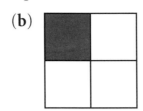   (b) 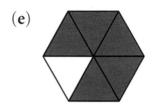   (c)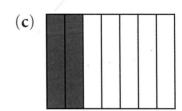

(d) 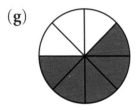   (e) 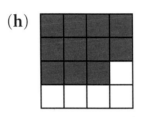   (f)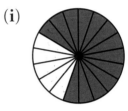

(g) 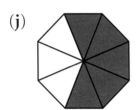   (h) 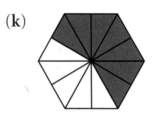   (i)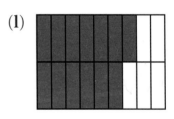

(j)   (k)   (l)

6 Look at the group of stars.
   (a) How many stars are there in total?
   (b) What fraction of the stars are red?
   (c) What fraction of the stars are green?
   (d) What fraction of the stars are NOT blue?

W You need Worksheet **5.2** for question **7**.

5.2 Equal fractions using shapes

Two squares the same size are shown.

On each square the red sections are the same size.

So $\frac{1}{2}$ must be the same as $\frac{2}{4}$.

These fractions are equal.

$$\frac{1}{2} = \frac{2}{4}$$

$\frac{1}{2}$		
$\frac{1}{2}$		

	$\frac{1}{4}$	$\frac{1}{4}$
	$\frac{1}{4}$	$\frac{1}{4}$

Exercise 5.2

1 In each pair of shapes the shaded sections are the same size.
Write the equal fractions.

(a)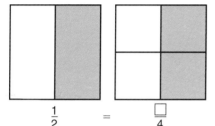

$$\frac{1}{2} = \frac{\square}{4}$$

(b)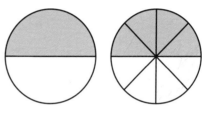

(c)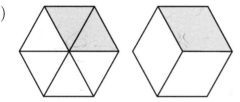

(d)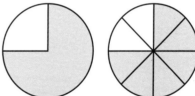

(e)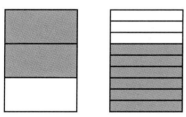

(f)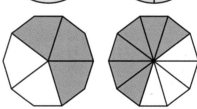

V You need Worksheet **5.3** for questions **2** and **3**.

5.3 Equal fractions

$\xrightarrow{\times 2}$

$$\frac{1}{5} = \frac{2}{10}$$

$\xleftarrow{\times 2}$

$\xrightarrow{\times 5}$

$$\frac{2}{3} = \frac{10}{15}$$

$\xleftarrow{\times 5}$

$\frac{1}{5}$ and $\frac{2}{10}$ are equivalent fractions.

$\frac{2}{3}$ and $\frac{10}{15}$ are equivalent fractions.

Exercise 5.3

W You need Worksheet **5.4** for question **1**.

2 Copy and complete:

(**a**)
$$\frac{1}{2} = \frac{4}{\square}$$
×4 (top), ×4 (bottom)

(**b**)
$$\frac{1}{3} = \frac{4}{\square}$$
×4 (top), ×4 (bottom)

(**c**)
$$\frac{1}{4} = \frac{\square}{20}$$
×5 (top), ×5 (bottom)

(**d**)
$$\frac{1}{5} = \frac{4}{\square}$$
×4 (top), ×4 (bottom)

(**e**)
$$\frac{1}{3} = \frac{\square}{21}$$
×7 (top), ×7 (bottom)

(**f**)
$$\frac{2}{3} = \frac{\square}{6}$$
×2 (top), ×2 (bottom)

(**g**)
$$\frac{3}{\square} = \frac{9}{15}$$
×3 (top), ×3 (bottom)

(**h**)
$$\frac{7}{\square} = \frac{21}{24}$$
×3 (top), ×3 (bottom)

(**i**)
$$\frac{6}{\square} = \frac{36}{42}$$
×6 (top), ×6 (bottom)

(**j**)
$$\frac{13}{\square} = \frac{39}{42}$$
×3 (top), ×3 (bottom)

5.4 Fractions of a quantity

Remember To find a fraction of a quantity, divide by the number on the bottom of the fraction.

To find $\frac{1}{2}$ divide by 2. | To find $\frac{1}{4}$ divide by 4. | To find $\frac{1}{5}$ divide by 5. | To find $\frac{1}{9}$ divide by 9.

Example 1

Calculate $\frac{1}{3}$ of 15 kg

$$\frac{1}{3} \text{ of } 15 = 15 \div 3$$
$$= 5$$

So $\frac{1}{3}$ of 15 kg = **5 kg**

Example 2

Use a calculator to find $\frac{1}{9}$ of £108

$$\frac{1}{9} \text{ of } 108 = 108 \div 9 = 12$$

So $\frac{1}{9}$ of £108 = **£12**

Exercise 5.4

1 Calculate:

(**a**) $\frac{1}{3}$ of 15p   (**b**) $\frac{1}{2}$ of 30 g   (**c**) $\frac{1}{4}$ of 16€   (**d**) $\frac{1}{5}$ of 30 ml

(**e**) $\frac{1}{2}$ of £24   (**f**) $\frac{1}{3}$ of 27 cm   (**g**) $\frac{1}{4}$ of £48   (**h**) $\frac{1}{6}$ of 18 m

(**i**) $\frac{1}{7}$ of \$14   (**j**) $\frac{1}{9}$ of £36   (**k**) $\frac{1}{10}$ of 120p   (**l**) $\frac{1}{5}$ of £125

(**m**) $\frac{1}{8}$ of 16 litres (**n**) $\frac{1}{3}$ of 36€   (**o**) $\frac{1}{2}$ of £3   (**p**) $\frac{1}{2}$ of 15 mm

2 Use a calculator to find:

(**a**) $\frac{1}{8}$ of 120 kg   (**b**) $\frac{1}{10}$ of 340 g   (**c**) $\frac{1}{9}$ of 369 ml   (**d**) $\frac{1}{12}$ of 2400p

(**e**) $\frac{1}{20}$ of £640   (**f**) $\frac{1}{100}$ of 10 000   (**g**) $\frac{1}{7}$ of 770 m   (**h**) $\frac{1}{11}$ of 242p

(**i**) $\frac{1}{9}$ of £981   (**j**) $\frac{1}{15}$ of 60 kg   (**k**) $\frac{1}{100}$ of 6000   (**l**) $\frac{1}{2}$ of £5

3 Thirty pupils enter a classroom.
$\frac{1}{3}$ of the pupils are girls.
How many pupils are girls?

5.5 Fractions and decimals

$\frac{1}{2}$ means $1 \div 2$

$$\frac{1}{2} = \boxed{1}\ \boxed{\div}\ \boxed{2}\ =\ \boxed{0.5}$$

Example   Write each fraction as a decimal.

(**a**) $\frac{1}{4}$ (**b**) $\frac{2}{5}$

$\qquad\quad 1\ \div\ 4 \qquad\qquad\qquad 2\ \div\ 5$

$\qquad\quad \boxed{1}\ \boxed{\div}\ \boxed{4} \qquad\qquad \boxed{2}\ \boxed{\div}\ \boxed{5}$

$\qquad\qquad = \mathbf{0.25} \qquad\qquad\qquad = \mathbf{0.4}$

Exercise 5.5

1 Write each fraction as a decimal:

(**a**) $\frac{1}{8}$ (**b**) $\frac{1}{10}$ (**c**) $\frac{1}{20}$ (**d**) $\frac{1}{100}$

(**e**) $\frac{3}{4}$ (**f**) $\frac{4}{5}$ (**g**) $\frac{5}{8}$ (**h**) $\frac{7}{10}$

(**i**) $\frac{3}{8}$ (**j**) $\frac{1}{20}$ (**k**) $\frac{1}{40}$ (**l**) $\frac{9}{10}$

(**m**) $\frac{3}{10}$ (**n**) $\frac{7}{20}$ (**o**) $\frac{17}{40}$ (**p**) $\frac{1}{3}$

2 Copy and complete the table below.

Fraction	$\frac{1}{4}$	$\frac{1}{2}$	$\frac{3}{4}$	$\frac{1}{5}$	$\frac{2}{5}$	$\frac{3}{5}$	$\frac{4}{5}$	$\frac{1}{10}$
Decimal	0·25							

These are common fractions and decimals.

W You need Worksheets **5.5** and **5.6** for questions 3 and 4.

Review exercise 5

1 Write the fraction of red pens.

2 (a) Write the total number of shapes.
   (b) Write the fraction of shapes that are squares.
   (c) Write the fraction of shapes that are circles.

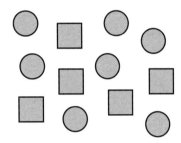

3 (a) Draw a square and shade $\frac{1}{2}$.
   (b) Draw another square exactly the same size and shade $\frac{1}{4}$.

4 Write the equal shaded fraction for each pair of shapes.

(a)    (b)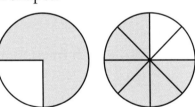

5 Copy and complete:
   (a) $\frac{1}{2} = \frac{4}{\square}$ (b) $\frac{2}{3} = \frac{6}{\square}$ (c) $\frac{2}{\square} = \frac{10}{25}$

6 Calculate:
   (a) $\frac{1}{2}$ of £20   (b) $\frac{1}{5}$ of 40 kg
   (c) $\frac{1}{7}$ of 42 m   (d) $\frac{1}{2}$ of £7

 7 Use a calculator to change each fraction to a decimal.
   (a) $\frac{1}{2}$ (b) $\frac{1}{4}$ (c) $\frac{1}{5}$
   (d) $\frac{1}{8}$ (e) $\frac{2}{5}$ (f) $\frac{19}{20}$

Summary

Review

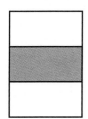

$\frac{1}{3}$ of the shape is shaded red.

$\frac{2}{3}$ of the shape is unshaded.

Equal fractions

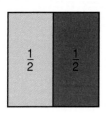

$\frac{1}{2} = \frac{2}{4}$

Fractions of a quantity

To find $\frac{1}{2}$ divide by 2.   To find $\frac{1}{4}$ divide by 4.   To find $\frac{1}{5}$ divide by 5.   To find $\frac{1}{9}$ divide by 9.

Changing a fraction to a decimal

$\frac{1}{2} = \boxed{1} \boxed{\div} \boxed{2} = \boxed{0 \cdot 5}$

$\frac{1}{2} = 0 \cdot 5$

6 Symmetry and tessellations

In this chapter you will review line symmetry and learn about rotational symmetry and tessellations.

6.1 Line symmetry

The dotted line cuts the shape in half so that one half will fold exactly on to the other.

This is called a **line of symmetry**.

Exercise 6.1

W You need Worksheets **6.1** to **6.3** for questions **1** to **4**.

5 Which of these shapes could have a line of symmetry?

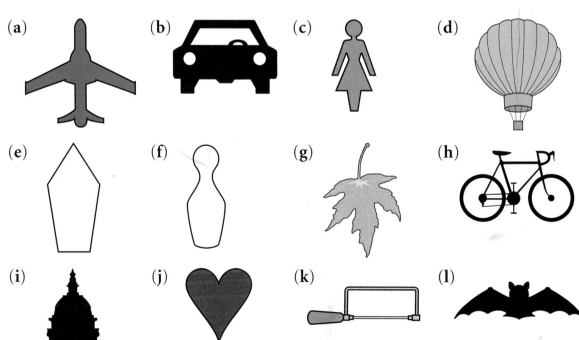

(a)   (b)   (c)   (d)

(e)   (f)   (g)   (h)

(i)   (j)   (k)   (l)

6 Copy each shape on squared paper and draw on the line of symmetry.

(**a**)

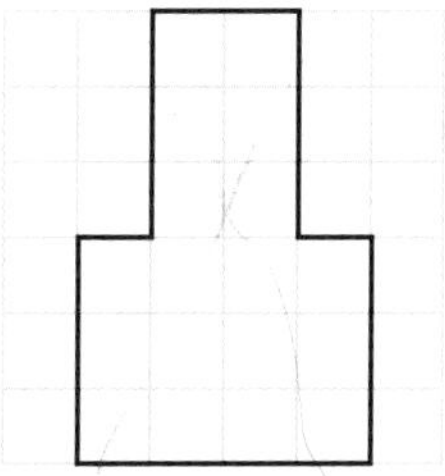

(**b**)

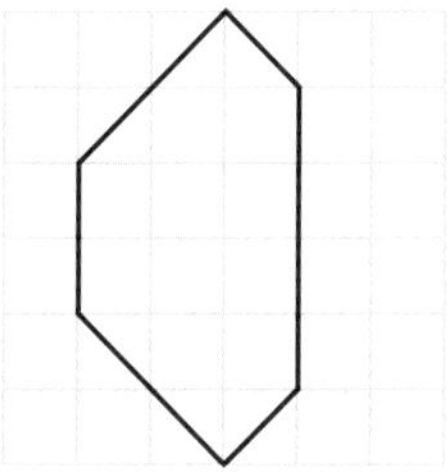

(**c**)

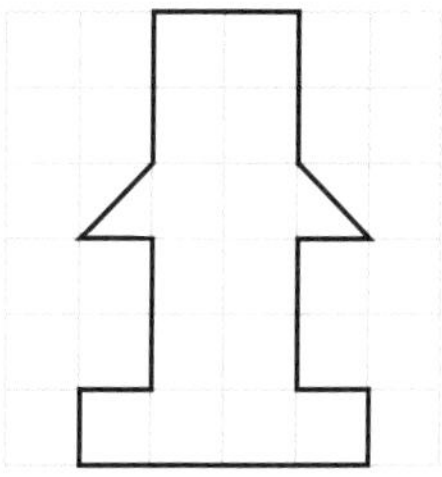

7 Copy and complete each diagram so that the dotted line is a line of symmetry.

(**a**)

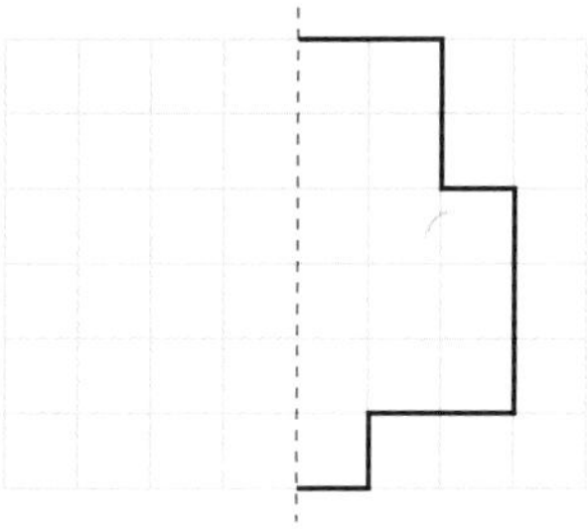

(**b**)

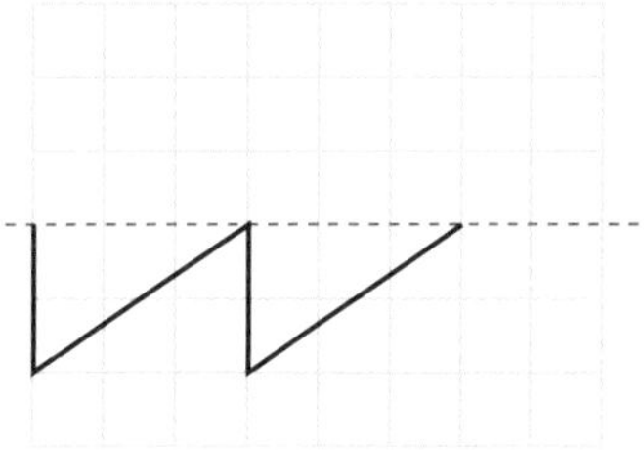

(**c**)

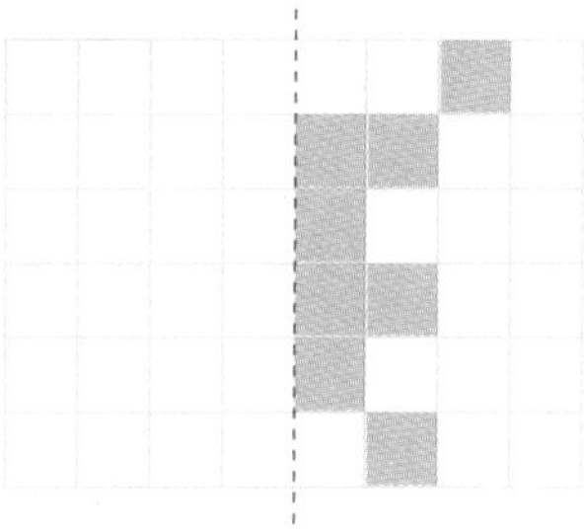

(**d**)

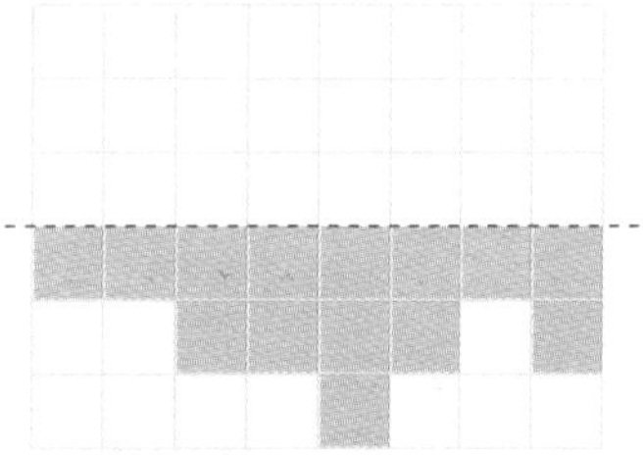

(**e**)

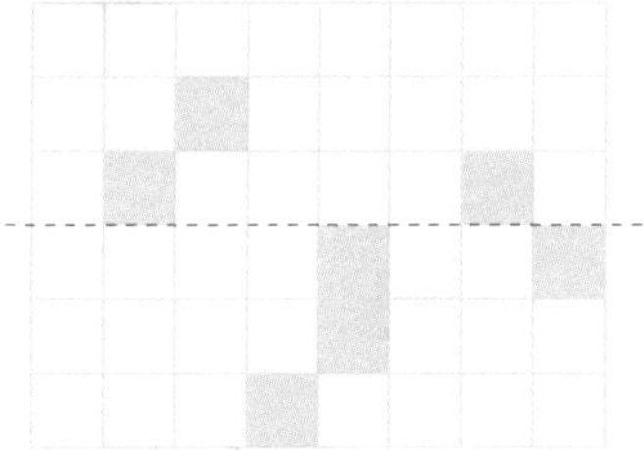

(**f**)

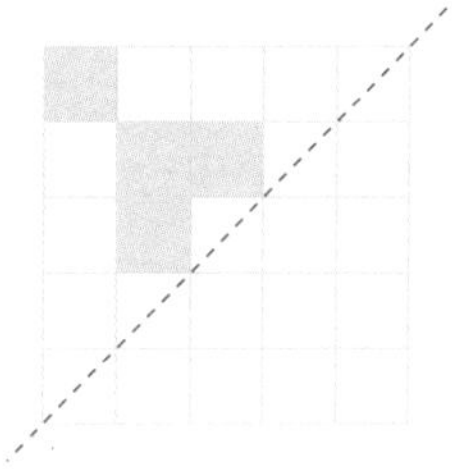

8 Which of these flags have one line of symmetry?

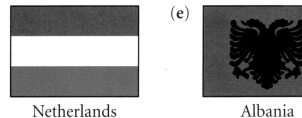

(**a**) Brazil

(**b**) St Lucia

(**c**) Denmark

(**d**) Netherlands

(**e**) Albania

(**f**) Canada

6.2 Lines of symmetry

Some shapes have more than one line of symmetry.

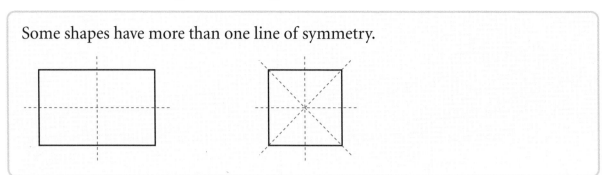

Exercise 6.2

You need scissors for this exercise.

W You need Worksheets **6.4** and **6.5** for questions **1** and **2**.

3 Copy these shapes on squared paper and draw on all lines of symmetry.

(a) (b) (c)

(d) (e)

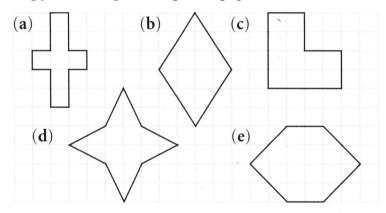

W You may use Worksheet **6.6** for question **4**.

4 How many lines of symmetry do the flags below have?

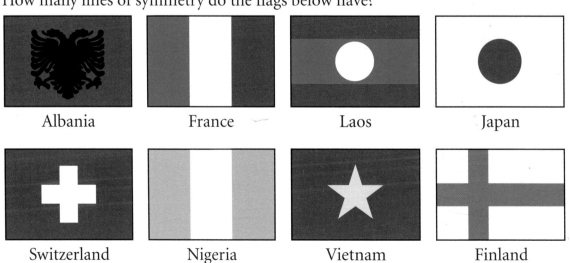

Albania   France   Laos   Japan

Switzerland   Nigeria   Vietnam   Finland

5 How many lines of symmetry does each shape have?

(a)

(b)

(c)

(d)

(e)

(f)

(g)

(h)

6 Copy and complete each diagram so that the dotted lines are lines of symmetry.

(a)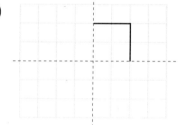

(b)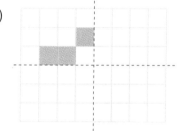

6.3 Half-turn symmetry

A shape that may be rotated about its central point to fit its own outline has rotational symmetry.

A rectangle given a half-turn about its centre fits its own outline.

This is called **half-turn symmetry**.

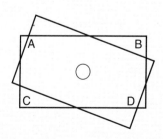

Exercise 6.3

You will need tracing paper for this exercise.

1 Trace each shape and use the tracing to decide if the shape has half-turn symmetry.

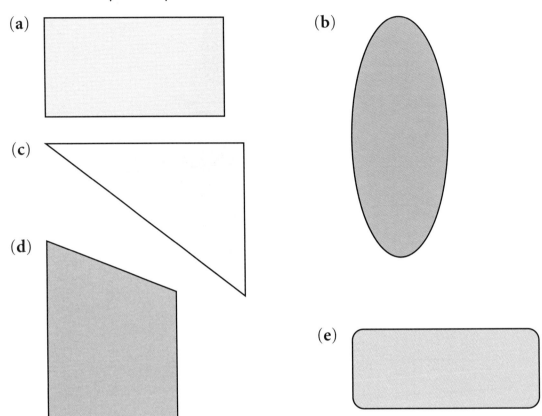

(a)

(b)

(c)

(d)

(e)

2 Which of the shapes below has half-turn symmetry? You may need tracing paper.

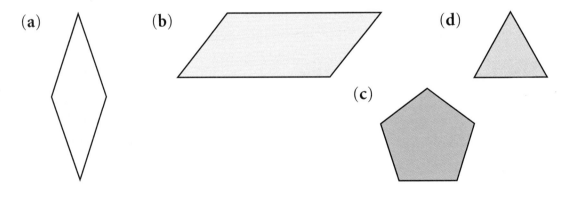

(a)

(b)

(d)

(c)

3 Which of these pictures has half-turn symmetry?

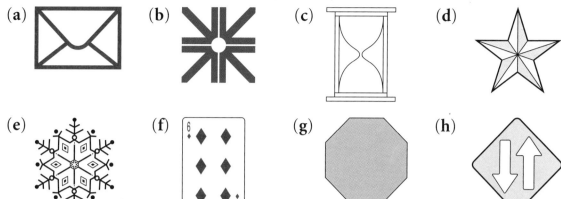

(a)   (b)   (c)   (d)

(e)   (f)   (g)   (h)

4 Write the capital letters of the alphabet that have half-turn symmetry.

A B C D E F G H I J K L M
N O P Q R S T U V W X Y Z

5 Which of the flags below have half-turn symmetry?

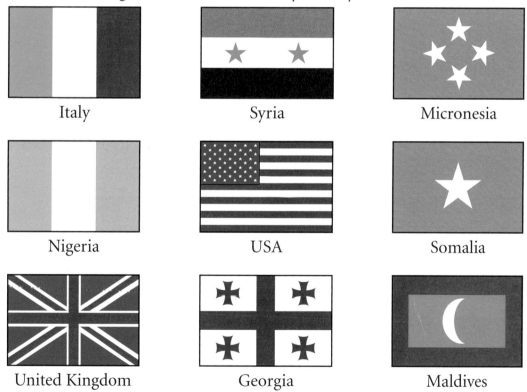

Italy   Syria   Micronesia

Nigeria   USA   Somalia

United Kingdom   Georgia   Maldives

6 List any other pictures, symbols or signs you can think of that have half-turn symmetry.

W You need Worksheet **6.7** for question **7**.

6.4 Tessellations

When shapes are fitted together with no gaps or overlaps we call the pattern a tessellation. You will look at tessellations using shapes that are the same size and shape.

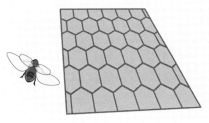 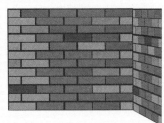 

Exercise 6.4

You will need squared and triangular dotted paper.

1 Make a list of where you might see examples of tessellations.

W You need Worksheets **6.8** to **6.10** for question **2**.

3 Using square dotted paper, copy and complete these tessellations using 12 tiles.

(**a**) 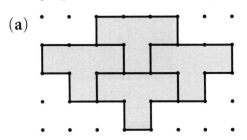 (**b**)

4 Using triangular dotted paper, copy and complete these tessellations using 12 tiles.

(**a**)  (**b**)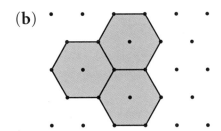

W You need Worksheet **6.11** for question **5**.

5 The Crazy Paving Company are designing their new catalogue.

(**a**) Continue these paving designs on Worksheet **6.11**.

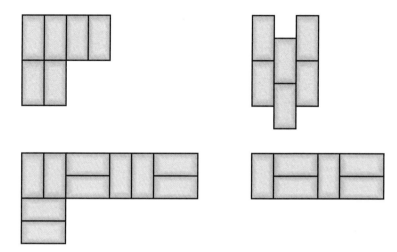

(**b**) Draw another design of your own using rectangles.

6 Do these shapes tessellate? Explain your answer.

(**a**) 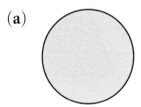   (**b**)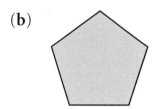

W You need Worksheet **6.12** for question **7**.

7 Use Worksheet **6.12** to draw a tessellation using this cat tile.

   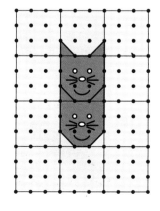

Review exercise 6

1 Copy and complete each diagram so that the dotted line is a line of symmetry.

(a)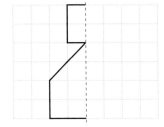

(b)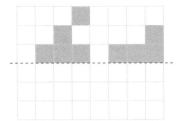

(c)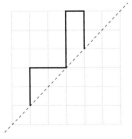

(d)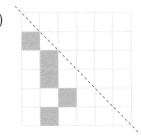

2 Copy these shapes and draw all the lines of symmetry.

(a)

(b)

(c)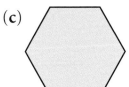

(d)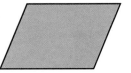

3 How many lines of symmetry does each sign have?

(a)

(b)

(c)

(d)

(e)

(f)

(g)

(h)

4 Which of these pictures have half-turn symmetry?

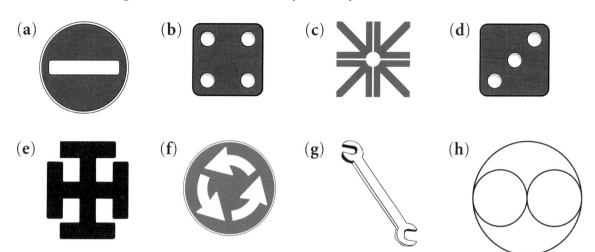

(a)   (b)   (c)   (d)

(e)   (f)   (g)   (h)

5 Using square dotted paper copy and complete these tessellations using 12 tiles.

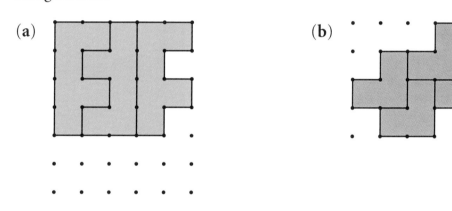

(a)   (b)

Summary

Line symmetry

The dotted line cuts the shape in half
so that one half will fold exactly on to the other.

This is called a **line of symmetry**.

Some shapes have more than one line of symmetry.

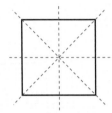

Half-turn symmetry

A shape that may be rotated about its central point
to fit its own outline has rotational symmetry.

A rectangle given a half-turn about its centre fits
its own outline.

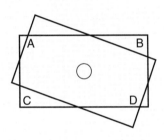

This is called **half-turn symmetry**.

Tessellations

When shapes are fitted together with no gaps or overlaps, we call the pattern a
tessellation.

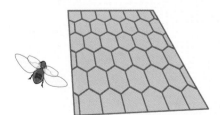
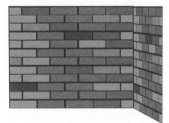

7 Percentages

In this chapter you will learn about percentages, decimals and fractions and calculate percentage of a quantity.

7.1 Understanding percentages

Percentage (%) means out of 100.

Example 1
This diagram has 40 out of 100 equal parts shaded.

Write the percentage that is shaded.

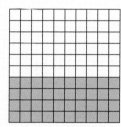

$$\frac{40}{100} = \textbf{40\%}$$

Example 2
Write $\frac{83}{100}$ as a percentage.

$$\frac{83}{100} = \textbf{83\%}$$

Example 3
Write 47% as a fraction.

$$47\% = \frac{47}{100}$$

Exercise 7.1

1 For each diagram, write the fraction out of 100 and the percentage shaded.

(a)

(b)

(c)

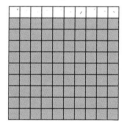 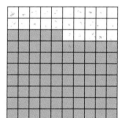 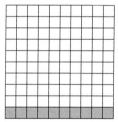

(d)

(e)

(f)

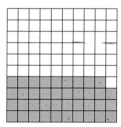 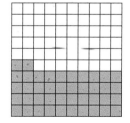 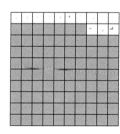

(g)

(h)

(i)

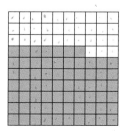 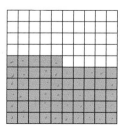 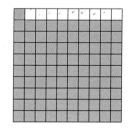

2 (**a**) Copy the square grid shown.
    (10 by 10 squares.)

(**b**) Colour 20% of your grid.

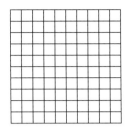

W You need Worksheet **7.1** for question **3**.

4 Write each fraction as a percentage: $\frac{78}{100} = 78\%$

(**a**) $\frac{14}{100}$ (**b**) $\frac{36}{100}$ (**c**) $\frac{87}{100}$ (**d**) $\frac{63}{100}$

(**e**) $\frac{51}{100}$ (**f**) $\frac{29}{100}$ (**g**) $\frac{91}{100}$ (**h**) $\frac{33}{100}$

(**i**) $\frac{99}{100}$ (**j**) $\frac{17}{100}$ (**k**) $\frac{10}{100}$ (**l**) $\frac{50}{100}$

5 Write each percentage as a fraction out of 100: $29\% = \frac{29}{100}$

(**a**) 23%   (**b**) 37%   (**c**) 63%   (**d**) 89%

(**e**) 11%   (**f**) 53%   (**g**) 67%   (**h**) 27%

(**i**) 99%   (**j**) 19%   (**k**) 1%   (**l**) 9%

7.2 Percentage of a quantity

 $50\% = \frac{1}{2}$ $25\% = \frac{1}{4}$ $10\% = \frac{1}{10}$

Example

(**a**) Find 50% of £40

50% of 40 $= \frac{1}{2} \times 40$

$= 20$

50% of £40 is **£20**

(**b**) Find 25% of 24 kg

25% of 24 $= \frac{1}{4} \times 24$

$= 6$

25% of 24 kg is **6 kg**

(**c**) Find 10% of 50p

10% of 50 $= \frac{1}{10} \times 50$

$= 5$

10% of 50p is **5p**

Exercise 7.2

1 Find:

(**a**) 50% of £60   (**b**) 50% of 24 kg   (**c**) 50% of 300p

(**d**) 25% of £40   (**e**) 25% of 16 cm   (**f**) 25% of 32 ml

(**g**) 10% of £30   (**h**) 10% of 70 g   (**i**) 10% of 600p

2 Find:

    (**a**) 50% of £90   (**b**) 25% of 80 kg   (**c**) 10% of 250p

    (**d**) 25% of £64   (**e**) 10% of 160 m   (**f**) 50% of 36 ℓ

    (**g**) 10% of £300   (**h**) 25% of 60 kg   (**i**) 50% of £3

3 (**a**) Gary had £40.
      He spent 50% of his money
      on a computer game.
      How much did the game cost?

   (**b**) Sharon had £84.
      She spent 25% of her money
      on a new blouse.
      How much did the blouse cost?

   (**c**) Jack had £30.
      He spent 10% on sweets.
      How much did Jack have left?

7.3 Percentages and decimals

Remember $17\% = \frac{17}{100}$

                  $\frac{17}{100}$ means 17 ÷ 100 = 0·17 $\boxed{17}\ \boxed{\div}\ \boxed{100}\ \boxed{=}\ \boxed{0\text{·}17}$

                  $\frac{23}{100}$ means 23 ÷ 100 = 0·23 $\boxed{23}\ \boxed{\div}\ \boxed{100}\ \boxed{=}\ \boxed{0\text{·}23}$

        A percentage may be written as a decimal.

Example   Write 2% as a decimal.

        $\boxed{2}\ \boxed{\div}\ \boxed{100}\ \boxed{=}\ \boxed{0\text{·}02}$

        2% = 0·02

Exercise 7.3

1 Use a calculator to change each percentage into a decimal:

    (**a**) 41%   (**b**) 57%   (**c**) 81%   (**d**) 77%

    (**e**) 99%   (**f**) 13%   (**g**) 16%   (**h**) 82%

    (**i**) 28%   (**j**) 38%·   (**k**) 44%   (**l**) 100%

2 Change each of these into decimals:

(**a**) 1%   (**b**) 2%   (**c**) 3%

(**d**) 4%   (**e**) 5%   (**f**) 6%

(**g**) 7%   (**h**) 8%   (**i**) 9%

3 Change each of these into decimals:

(**a**) 10%   (**b**) 20%   (**c**) 30%

(**d**) 40%   (**e**) 50%   (**f**) 60%

(**g**) 70%   (**h**) 80%   (**i**) 90%

7.4 Percentages using a calculator

Example   Calculate 17% of £400   ⌈ 17% = 0·17 ⌋

17% of 400 = ⌈0·17⌋ × ⌈400⌋ = ⌈68⌋

So 17% of £400 is **£68.**

Exercise 7.4

1 Calculate:

(**a**) 17% of £500   (**b**) 25% of £640   (**c**) 35% of 200 kg

(**d**) 40% of 320 cm   (**e**) 80% of £80   (**f**) 60% of 700 g

(**g**) 42% of 200p   (**h**) 85% of 600 m   (**i**) 99% of 3000 km

2 Calculate: ⌈ 7% = 0.07 ⌋

(**a**) 7% of £200   (**b**) 5% of £600   (**c**) 3% of 200 g

(**d**) 8% of 320 kg   (**e**) 6% of £300   (**f**) 9% of 500 mm

(**g**) 2% of $2000   (**h**) 4% of 650€   (**i**) 1% of £3000

3 Calculate:

(**a**) 50% of £19   (**b**) 36% of £60

(**c**) 45% of £250   (**d**) 88% of £90

(**e**) 62% of £1540

> **Remember** when dealing with money there must be two numbers after the decimal point.

4 Keri had £125.
She spent 50% of her money on horse riding.
How much did Keri spend on horse riding?

5 Dan had £6.
He spent 10% on comics.
How much did Dan spend on comics?

6 Beth had £82.
She spent 25% on a CD player.
How much did Beth spend on the CD player?

7 Jen had £200.
Jen spent 75% of her money on holiday.
How much did Jen spend on holiday?

8 Chas had £200.
He spent 80% of his money on holiday.
(**a**) How much did Chas spend on holiday?
(**b**) How much did Chas have left?

9 Pete spent 30% of his £80 savings on swimming lessons.
(**a**) How much did Pete spend?
(**b**) How much did Pete have left?

10 Zak spent 25% of the £22 in his piggy bank on chocolate.
(**a**) How much did Zak spend on chocolate?
(**b**) How much did Zak have left?
(**c**) Zak then spent 10% of the money he had left on a
magazine. How much did Zak now have left?

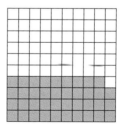

Review exercise 7

1 Look at the diagram.
(**a**) Write the fraction shaded.
(**b**) Write the percentage shaded.
(**c**) Write the percentage not shaded.

2 Write each fraction as a percentage:
(**a**) $\frac{33}{100}$ (**b**) $\frac{91}{100}$ (**c**) $\frac{70}{100}$ (**d**) $\frac{3}{100}$

3 Write each percentage as a fraction:
(**a**) 23%   (**b**) 71%   (**c**) 80%   (**d**) 9%

4 Find:

    (**a**) 50% of £24   (**b**) 25% of 32 kg

    (**c**) 10% of 600 m   (**d**) 50% of £3

 5 Karen has £125 in the bank.
She spends 25% of her money on clothes.
How much does Karen have left?

6 Change each of these percentages into a decimal:

    (**a**) 47%   (**b**) 87%   (**c**) 40%   (**d**) 3%

7 Use a calculator to find:

    (**a**) 16% of £700   (**b**) 8% of 450 kg

Summary

Percentage

Percentage (%) means out of 100.

This diagram has 40 out of 100 equal parts shaded.

$\frac{40}{100} = 40\%$

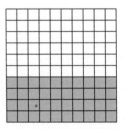

Percentage as a fraction

$50\% = \frac{1}{2}$ $25\% = \frac{1}{4}$ $10\% = \frac{1}{10}$

Percentage as a decimal

$\frac{17}{100}$ means $17 \div 100 = 0{\cdot}17$ $\boxed{17}\,\boxed{\div}\,\boxed{100}\,\boxed{=}\,\boxed{0{\cdot}17}$

Percentage using a calculator

Example   Calculate 17% of £400 $\boxed{17\% = 0{\cdot}17}$

                 17% of 400 = 0·17 × 400 = 68

                 So 17% of £400 is **£68**.

8 Measurement

In this chapter you will learn how to use metric units and calculate with them.

8.1 Reading scales

Before measuring you must be able to read the scale. Be careful to check the value of each space.

Each space stands for 1 cm.

The wingspan is **6 cm.**

Each space stands for 1 mm.

The wingspan is **45 mm.**

Each space stands for 500 g.

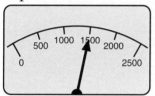

The weight is **1500 g.**

Each space stands for 10 ml.

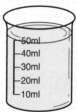

The volume is **50 ml.**

Exercise 8.1

W You need Worksheet **8.1** for question **1.**

2 (**a**) What does each space represent on the ruler below?
   (**b**) What is the reading for each pointer?

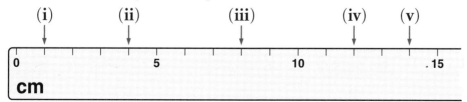

3 (**a**) What does each small space represent on the ruler?
(**b**) What is the reading for each pointer?

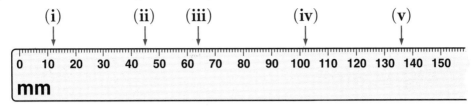

4 (**a**) What does each space represent?
(**b**) What is the reading at each pointer?

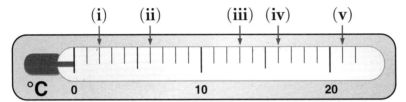

5 (**a**) What does each space represent?
(**b**) What is the reading at each pointer?

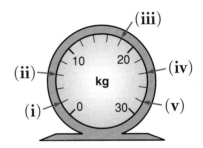

6 (**a**) What does each space represent?
(**b**) How much is in each beaker?

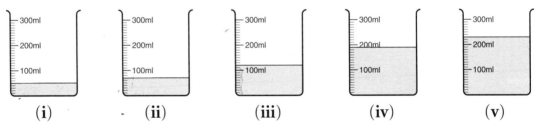

7 (**a**) What does each space represent?
(**b**) How much is in each beaker?

8.2 Estimating and measuring length

You may use common objects to estimate measurements before measuring accurately.

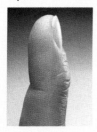

The thickness of a fingernail is about 1 millimetre.

The width of your smallest finger is about 1 centimetre.

The height of a door is about 2 metres.

The length of the Forth Rail Bridge is about $2\frac{1}{2}$ kilometres.

Exercise 8.2

W You need Worksheets **8.2** and **8.3** for questions **1** to **3**.

4 For each butterfly: (**a**) estimate the wingspan
                         (**b**) measure the wingspan.

(**i**)

(**ii**)

(**iii**)

8.3 Shorter lengths

Shorter lengths are often measured using millimetres.

10 millimetres = 1 centimetre

10 mm = 1 cm

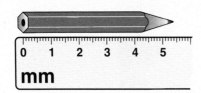

The length of this pencil is

5 cm 4 mm   or   5·4 cm   or   54 mm

5 cm 4 mm = 5·4 cm = 54 mm

Exercise 8.3

1 Measure each pencil and write the length in:

(**a**) centimetres and millimetres   (**b**) centimetres   (**c**) millimetres.

(**i**)

(**ii**)

(**iii**)

(**iv**)

(**v**)

2 Write the length of the pencils in question **1** in order of size, using centimetres. Start with the shortest.

3 Write each of the following lists in order of size, shortest first.

(**a**) 4·5 cm,   5·4 cm,   3·2 cm,   6·1 cm

(**b**) 81 mm,   67 mm,   49 mm,   53 mm

(**c**) 3·5 cm,   3·8 cm,   3·1 cm,   3·7 cm

(**d**) 91 mm,   90 mm,   95 mm,   99 mm

4 Read the measurements from each ruler. Give your answer in:
   (**a**) centimetres and millimetres   (**b**) centimetres   (**c**) millimetres.

   (**i**)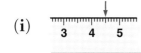

   (**ii**)

   (**iii**)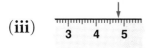

   (**iv**)

   (**v**)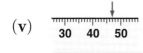

5 Write each of the following in centimetres.
   (**a**) 2 cm 5 mm   (**b**) 3 cm 4 mm   (**c**) 6 cm 2 mm   (**d**) 8 cm 7 mm
   (**e**) 99 mm   (**f**) 35 mm   (**g**) 28 mm   (**h**) 5 mm

6 Write each of the following in millimetres.
   (**a**) 5·3 cm   (**b**) 2·1 cm   (**c**) 6·8 cm   (**d**) 7·3 cm
   (**e**) 0·8 cm   (**f**) 9·8 cm   (**g**) 5 cm 9 mm   (**h**) 8 cm 6 mm

8.4 Longer lengths

Remember
100 cm = 1 m

Curt's height is
1 metre 73 centimetres or 1·73 metres or 173 centimetres

1 m 73 cm = 1·73 m = 173 cm

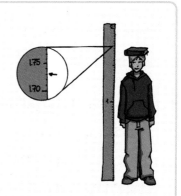

Exercise 8.4

1 (**a**) Write the height of each pupil in:

(**i**) metres and centimetres   (**ii**) metres   (**iii**) centimetres.

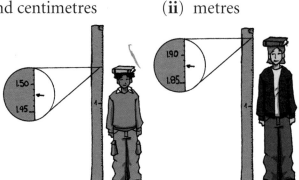

(**b**) Write the heights of all three pupils (including Curt on page 99) in order of size, using metres. Start with the shortest.

2 Write the following measurements in order of size, shortest first.

(**a**) 2·5 m,   1·4 m,   6·1 m,   3·4 m

(**b**) 4·65 m,   4·56 m,   4·91 m,   4·76 m

(**c**) 568 cm,   560 cm,   580 cm,   569 cm

(**d**) 7·19 m,   7·91 m,   7·1 m,   7·9 m

3 (**a**) Read the measurement from each measuring tape, in metres.

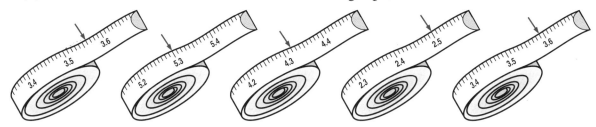

(**b**) Write the measurements in order of size, shortest first.

4 Write each of the following in metres.

(**a**) 3 m 45 cm   (**b**) 2 m 65 cm   (**c**) 7 m 13 cm   (**d**) 4 m 5 cm

(**e**) 2 m 50 cm   (**f**) 325 cm   (**g**) 206 cm   (**h**) 50 cm

5 Write each of the following in centimetres.

(**a**) 5 m   (**b**) 2·65 m   (**c**) 4·31 m   (**d**) 7·5 m

(**e**) 4 m 50 cm   (**f**) 3 m 60 cm   (**g**) 9 m 56 cm   (**h**) 6 m 8 cm

6 Write these lengths in order, starting with the longest.

3 m 16 cm,   324 cm,   3 m 37 cm,   3·09 m

8.5 Length and distance

The length of this piece of wood is 2·5 metres or 2 metres 500 millimetres or 2500 millimetres.

2·5 m = 2 m 500 mm = 2500 mm

1000 metres = 1 kilometre

1000 m = 1 km

The Royal Mile is 1 kilometre 600 metres long.

1 km 600 m = 1·6 km = 1600 m

Exercise 8.5

1 Write the length of each plank in:

(**a**) metres and millimetres   (**b**) millimetres   (**c**) metres.

(**i**)

0 10 20 30 40 50 60 70 80 90 100 110 120 130 140 150 160 170 180 190 200 210 220 230 240 250 cm

(**ii**)

0 10 20 30 40 50 60 70 80 90 100 110 120 130 140 150 160 170 180 190 200 210 220 230 240 250 cm

(**iii**)

0 10 20 30 40 50 60 70 80 90 100 110 120 130 140 150 160 170 180 190 200 210 220 230 240 250 cm

(**iv**)

0 10 20 30 40 50 60 70 80 90 100 110 120 130 140 150 160 170 180 190 200 210 220 230 240 250 cm

2 Write the lengths of the planks in question **1** in order of size, using metres. Start with the shortest.

3 Write each of the following in metres.

(**a**) 4000 mm   (**b**) 7000 mm   (**c**) 5000 mm   (**d**) 500 mm

(**e**) 2 m 500 mm   (**f**) 8 m 250 mm   (**g**) 5 m 750 mm   (**h**) 4 m 500 mm

4 Write each of the following in millimetres.

(**a**) 6 m   (**b**) 4 m   (**c**) 11 m   (**d**) 10 m

(**e**) 3 m 500 mm   (**f**) 6 m 500 mm   (**g**) 4 m 750 mm   (**h**) 0·5 m

5 (**a**) Write each distance from the Viewpoint, in kilometres.

(**b**) List the distances in order, longest first.

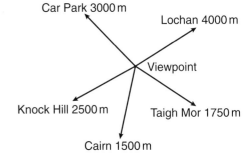

6 Write each of the following in kilometres.

(**a**) 4000 m   (**b**) 6000 m   (**c**) 2500 m   (**d**) 250 m

7 Write each of the following in metres.

(**a**) 3 km   (**b**) 8 km 250 m   (**c**) 2·5 km   (**d**) 8·75 m

8.6 Weight

> 1000 grammes (g) = 1 kilogramme (kg)
>
> 1000 kilogrammes (kg) = 1 tonne
>
> It is useful to estimate weights using common objects before measuring accurately.
>
> The weight of an A4 sheet of paper is about 5 grammes.
>
> The weight of a bag of sugar is 1 kilogramme.
>
> The weight of an average 15-year-old boy is about 50 kilogrammes.
>
> The weight of a bus is about 3 tonnes.

Exercise 8.6

1 Estimate your weight in kilogrammes.

2 Match the estimated weights with the objects given.

(**a**)   (**b**)    (**c**)    (**d**)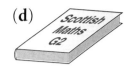

    1 kilogramme   40 kilogrammes   100 grammes   1 tonne

3 Which metric unit (tonnes, kilogrammes or grammes) should you use to measure the following weights:

(**a**) a newspaper   (**b**) a crate of cola   (**c**) an ipod

(**d**) your weight   (**e**) an oil tanker?

8.7 Measuring weight

The weight of this flour is
1 kilogramme 500 grammes or

1 kg 500 g = 1·5 kg = 1500 g

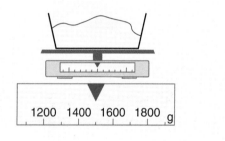

Exercise 8.7

1 Write the reading on each scale in kilogrammes.

(**a**) 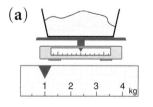   (**b**) 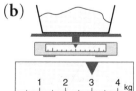   (**c**) 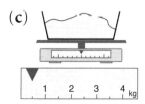   (**d**)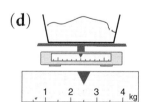

2 Write the weights from question **1** in grammes.

3 Write each of the following in kilogrammes.

(**a**) 5000 g   (**b**) 2500 g   (**c**) 3 kg 500 g   (**d**) 500 g

4 Write each of the following in grammes.
   (**a**) 7 kg   (**b**) 9 kg 500 g   (**c**) 4·5 kg   (**d**) 2·75 kg

5 Write each of the following in kilogrammes and grammes.
   (**a**) 6·5 kg   (**b**) 7500 g   (**c**) 10·5 kg   (**d**) 3·75 kg

6 Write the weights of the following dinosaurs in:
   (**a**) tonnes and kilogrammes   (**b**) tonnes.

(**i**)

Tyrannosaurus (tyrant lizard)
weight: 6400 kg

(**ii**)

Triceratops (three-horned face)
weight: 5400 kg

(**iii**)

Iguanodon (iguana tooth)
weight: 4500 kg

(**iv**)

Diplodocus (double beam)
weight: 10 600 kg

(**v**)

Brachiosaurus (arm lizard)
weight: 77 100 kg

(**vi**)

Ultrasaurus (extreme lizard)
weight: 136 000 kg

7 List the above dinosaurs in order of weight, starting with the heaviest.

8 Write each of the following in tonnes.
   (**a**) 5000 kg   (**b**) 6 tonnes 500 kg   (**c**) 2 tonnes 500 kg   (**d**) 3500 kg

9 Write each of the following in tonnes and kilogrammes.
   (**a**) 4·6 tonnes   (**b**) 7·5 tonnes   (**c**) 8721 kilogrammes   (**d**) 3·25 tonnes

8.8 Volume

Metric volume

1000 millilitres (ml) = 1 litre (ℓ)

Estimating volumes using common objects as a guide is a useful start before measuring accurately.

A teaspoon contains about 5 millilitres.
A cup contains about 200 millilitres.
A large bottle contains about 2 litres.
A school swimming pool contains about 30 million litres.

The volume of liquid in this measuring jug is
1 litre 525 millilitres or 1·525 litres or 1525 millilitres

1 ℓ 525 ml = 1.525 ℓ = 1525 ml

Exercise 8.8

1 Write down the volumes shown in each jug. Give your answer in litres and millilitres.

(**a**) 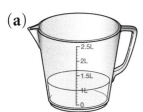 (**b**) 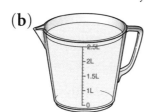 (**c**) 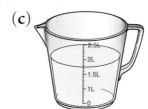 (**d**)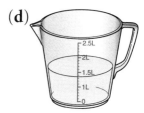

2 List the above volumes in order of size, smallest first.

3 Write each of the following in litres.
(**a**) 8000 ml (**b**) 3500 ml (**c**) 11 000 ml (**d**) 25 000 ml
(**e**) 7 ℓ 500 ml (**f**) 2 ℓ 500 ml (**g**) 6 ℓ 500 ml (**h**) 500 ml

4 Write each of the following in litres and millilitres.
(**a**) 7·5 ℓ (**b**) 3·5 ℓ (**c**) 5·5 ℓ (**d**) 10·5 ℓ
(**e**) 3000 ml (**f**) 1500 ml (**g**) 1250 ml (**h**) 500 ml

5 Write each of the following in millilitres.
(**a**) 4 ℓ (**b**) 6.5 ℓ (**c**) 8.5 ℓ (**d**) 9.75 ℓ
(**e**) 1 ℓ 500 ml (**f**) 8 ℓ 500 ml (**g**) 3 ℓ 250 ml (**h**) 2 ℓ 750 ml

8.9 Add and subtract with metric units

Example 1

A builder has 3 pieces of pipe as shown.
What is the total length?

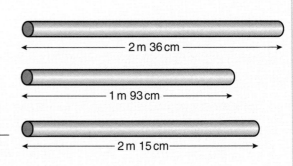

Pipe 1:   2 m 36 cm = 2·36 m

Pipe 2:   1 m 93 cm = 1·93 m

Pipe 3:   2 m 15 cm = 2·15 m

$$
\begin{array}{r}
2{\cdot}36\,m \\
1{\cdot}93\,m \\
+\ 2{\cdot}15\,m \\
\hline
6{\cdot}44\,m \\
\end{array}
$$

The total length is **6·44 m.**

Example 2

The petrol tank of Justine's car can hold 64 litres. When Justine fills the tank, the pump shows that she has bought 56 litres 500 millilitres.
How much was in the tank before she filled up?

Volume bought = 56 ℓ 500 ml = 56·5 ℓ

$$
\begin{array}{r}
6\,4{\cdot}0\,\ell \\
-56{\cdot}5\,\ell \\
\hline
7{\cdot}5\,\ell \\
\end{array}
$$

The volume before filling was **7·5 litres.**

Exercise 8.9

1 What is the total length of the pipes in each diagram?

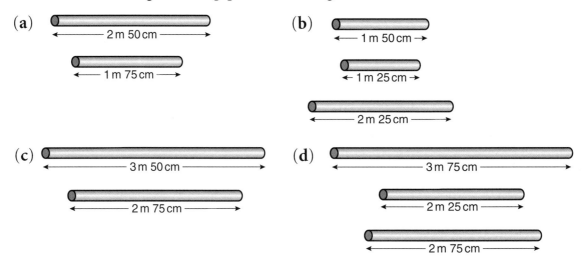

2 (**a**) Draw a rectangle 6 centimetres long and 4 centimetres broad.

(**b**) Calculate its perimeter.

3 Find the perimeter of each football pitch.

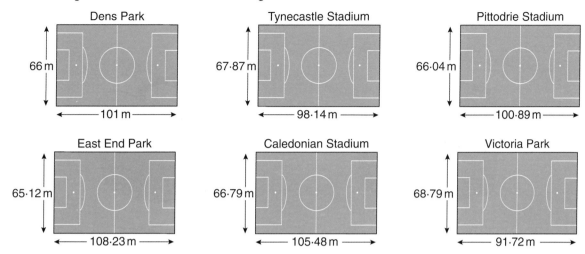

4 Find the perimeter of each rectangle.

(a) 3 cm 5 mm, 5 cm 5 mm

(b) 2 cm 5 mm, 2 cm 5 mm

5 (a) Collect the heights in metres of 5 pupils in your class.

(b) If all 5 were to lie down in a line, what would their total length be?

6 The number 42 bus travels along roads shown in this map. The distances between the stops are shown in metres. Calculate the total distance in kilometres between the following places.

(a) Portobello and Frederick Street

(b) Stockbridge and Silverknowes

(c) Cameron Toll and Crewe Toll

(d) Portobello and Silverknowes

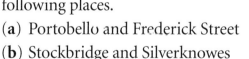

Silverknowes
1500 m
Crewe Toll
Stockbridge
750 m
2750 m
Frederick Street
3500 m
Portobello
500 m
Cameron Toll   4000 m

7 Calculate the amount remaining in each jug if a glass is filled in each case.

(a)   (b)   (c)

8 John weighed 74·5 kilogrammes. After a fitness programme, he found that he had lost 1500 grammes. What was his weight after the programme?

9 Find the total weight of these shopping baskets.

(**a**)

(**b**)

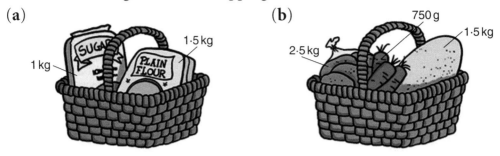

10 The diagrams show the long jump distances recorded in the senior school sports day. What is the difference between the longest and shortest jumps?

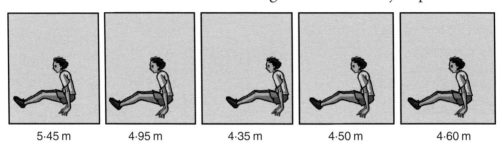

| 5·45 m | 4·95 m | 4·35 m | 4·50 m | 4·60 m |

8.10 Multiply and divide with metric units

Example 1

A car weighs 2 tonnes 500 kilogrammes.
What is the total weight of 6 cars?

1 car : 2 tonnes 500 kilogrammes = 2·5 tonnes

$$\begin{array}{r} 2.5 \\ \times\ 6 \\ \hline 15.0 \\ \tiny 3 \end{array}$$

Total weight = 2·5 × 6
$$= 15$$

The weight of 6 cars is **15 tonnes**.

Example 2

A jug contains 1·5 litres of orange juice. If the juice is shared equally among 3 glasses, how much will be in each glass?

Volume of jug = 1·5 ℓ = 1500 ml

$$\begin{array}{r} 500 \\ 3\overline{)1500} \end{array}$$

Volume of glass = 1500 ÷ 3
$$= 500$$

Each glass has **500 ml**.

Exercise 8.10

1 A car weighs 2 tonnes 500 kilogrammes. Find the weight of:

(**a**) 3 cars   (**b**) 5 cars   (**c**) 7 cars   (**d**) 9 cars   (**e**) 10 cars.

2 The length of a van is 3 metres 50 centimetres. Find the total length of:

(**a**) 4 vans   (**b**) 5 vans   (**c**) 8 vans   (**d**) 9 vans   (**e**) 10 vans.

3 A jug contains 1·5 litres of orange juice. How much is in each glass if it is shared equally among:

(**a**) 5 glasses   (**b**) 4 glasses   (**c**) 6 glasses   (**d**) 10 glasses?

4 A plank of wood is 3.6 metres long. How long will each piece be when it is cut into:

(**a**) 4 pieces   (**b**) 6 pieces   (**c**) 9 pieces   (**d**) 5 pieces?

Review exercise 8

1 (**a**) What does each space represent?

(**b**) What is the reading at each pointer?

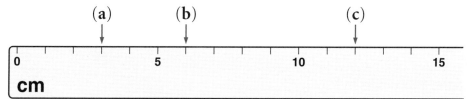

2 (**a**) What does each space represent?

(**b**) What is the reading at each pointer?

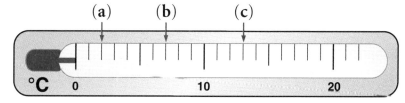

3 (**a**) Estimate the wingspan of the butterfly.

(**b**) Measure its wingspan.

4 Write each of the following in centimetres.

(**a**) 3 cm 5 mm   (**b**) 27 mm   (**c**) 5 cm 3 mm   (**d**) 42 mm

5 Write each of the following in millimetres.

(**a**) 6·2 cm   (**b**) 3 cm 7 mm   (**c**) 7·9 cm   (**d**) 5 cm 4 mm

6 Write each of the following in metres.
(**a**) 5 m 65 cm   (**b**) 425 cm   (**c**) 2 m 50 cm   (**d**) 375 cm

7 Write each of the following in centimetres.
(**a**) 6 m   (**b**) 7·53 m   (**c**) 6 m 95 cm   (**d**) 3·5 m

8 Write each of the following in metres.
(**a**) 8000 mm   (**b**) 9500 mm   (**c**) 7 m 500 mm   (**d**) 1500 mm

9 Write each of the following in millimetres.
(**a**) 7 m   (**b**) 3 m 500 mm   (**c**) 2·5 m   (**d**) 12 m

10 Write each of the following in kilogrammes.
(**a**) 6000 g   (**b**) 9 kg 500 g   (**c**) 4500 g   (**d**) 2500 g

11 Write each of the following in grammes.
(**a**) 8 kg   (**b**) 5 kg 500 g   (**c**) 3·5 kg   (**d**) 6·75 kg

12 Write each of the following in kilogrammes and grammes.
(**a**) 5·5 kg   (**b**) 7500 g   (**c**) 3·75 kg   (**d**) 10·5 kg

13 Write each of the following in litres.
(**a**) 6000 ml   (**b**) 8 ℓ 500 ml   (**c**) 12 000 ml   (**d**) 6500 ml

14 Write each of the following in litres and millilitres.
(**a**) 6·5 ℓ   (**b**) 2500 ml   (**c**) 9·5 ℓ   (**d**) 1·25 ℓ

15 Write each of the following in millilitres.
(**a**) 6 ℓ   (**b**) 7·5 ℓ   (**c**) 3·5 ℓ   (**d**) 5·75 ℓ

16 What is the total length of the rugs in each diagram?

(**a**)

1 m 75 cm   2 m

(**b**)

1 m 25 cm   2 m 25 cm

2 m 50 cm

17 Find the total weight of these shopping baskets.

(**a**

(**b**)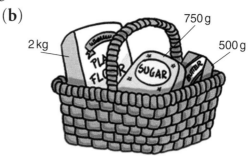

18 John drinks 1.5 litres of water every day. How much would he drink in:

(**a**) 5 days   (**b**) 7 days   (**c**) 9 days   (**d**) 10 days?

19 Mairi shares her chocolates among 5 friends. What weight would each receive if the box weighs:

(**a**) 200 g   (**b**) 500 g   (**c**) 1·5 kg   (**d**) 2·5 kg?

Summary

Length

10 millimetres (mm) = 1 centimetre (cm)
100 centimetres (cm) = 1 metre (m)
1000 millimetres (mm) = 1 metre (m)
1000 metres (m) = 1 kilometre (km)

Weight

1000 grammes (g) = 1 kilogramme (kg)
1000 kilogrammes (kg) = 1 tonne (t)

Volume

1000 millilitres (ml) = 1 litre (ℓ)

9 Time

In this chapter you will review time, learn to use the 24 hour clock and calculate time intervals.

9.1 12-hour clock

Remember
Time can be displayed on a clockface or on a digital clock.

These clocks both show fifteen minutes past eight or quarter past eight.

Exercise 9.1

W You need Worksheet **9.1** for questions **1, 2** and **3**.

4 Write in words the times shown on each clock.

(a)  (b)  (c)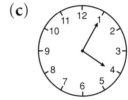

(d) 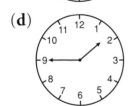 (e) 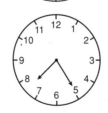 (f)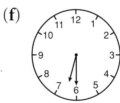

5 Write in words the times shown on each clock.

(a) 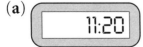 (b)  (c)

(d) 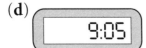 (e) 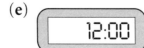 (f)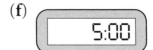

(g) 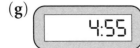 (h) 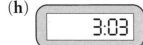 (i)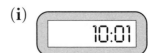

6 Draw the display of a digital clock showing these times:

(**a**) five past nine

(**b**) quarter past two

(**c**) half past six

(**d**) ten to seven

(**e**) twenty-five to twelve

(**f**) twenty past eleven.

9.2 a.m. and p.m.

Remember

6.15 a.m. means 6.15 in the morning

9.10 p.m. means 9.10 in the evening

a.m. means before 12 noon.

p.m. means after 12 noon.

Exercise 9.2

1 Write the times for these events using a.m. or p.m.

(**a**) evening meal 6.30

(**b**) afternoon tea 4.15

(**c**) morning coffee 10.45

(**d**) lunch 1.10

(**e**) supper 7.30

(**f**) breakfast 7.45.

2 Write these times in figures using a.m. or p.m.:

(**a**) half past six in the evening

(**b**) quarter past three in the afternoon

(**c**) ten to eleven in the morning

(**d**) eleven fifteen at night

(**e**) twenty to four in the morning

(**f**) twenty-five past eight at night

(**g**) ten thirty in the morning

(**h**) noon

(**i**) seven forty-five in the evening

(**j**) midnight.

3 Write the time for each event using a.m. or p.m.

(a) 7.30

(b) 1.30

(c) 2.15

(d) 10.30

(e) 11.10

(f) 4.30

(g) 7.45

(h) 11.20

(i) 9.30

9.3 24-hour clock

Times may be written using the 24-hour clock.
After 12 noon, the hours are numbered 13, 14, 15…
up to 24.

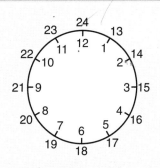

12-hour times	24-hour times
5.30 a.m.	05 30
10.15 a.m.	10 15
12 noon	12 00
5.20 p.m.	17 20
9.06 p.m.	21 06
12 midnight	24 00 or 00 00

> Use four figures for
> 24-hour times.

Example 1 Write each time using the 24-hour clock.
  (a) 7.20 a.m.   (b) 10.15 p.m.
  (a) **07 20**   (b) **22 15**

> For p.m. times, add 12
> to the number of hours.

Example 2 Write each time using the 12-hour clock.
  (a) 08 30   (b) 16 45
  (a) **8.30 a.m.**   (b) **4.45 p.m.**

Exercise 9.3

N You need Worksheet **9.2** for questions **1** and **2**.

3 Susan's travel plan shows these times.

Write her list in 24-hour clock notation.

> Glasgow   8 a.m.
> Edinburgh   9.30 a.m.
> Newcastle   12.15 p.m.
> Durham   3.20 p.m.
> York   7.54 p.m.

4 Copy and complete the table.

12-hour time	4.30 a.m.	2.15 p.m.		3.05 a.m.	
24-hour time			17 35		21 10

5 Michael is setting his digital alarm clock for 7.25 p.m.
Which of these is the correct setting?

  A   07 25   **B**   17 25   **C**   19 25

6 At the airport, Derek sees three flights listed for London.
His flight goes at 5.15 p.m.
Which is his flight number?

Flight no.	Departure time
GLX231	15 15
LFH519	17 15
KLN211	18 15

7 Sam must be at work by 2.30 p.m.
His train arrives at 14 45. Will he be on time?

W You need Worksheet **9.3** for questions **8** and **9**.

10 On his bus timetable Jeremias sees the times listed.
Write the list using the 12-hour clock.

Hamburg	09 15
Lubeck	11 20
Rostock	13 05
Stralsund	14 25

11 Jana finishes work at 4.30 p.m.
The clock in his office shows 16 35.
Can he leave work? Explain your answer.

12 Colin must be in Glasgow by 5.15 p.m.
The train he is on arrives in Glasgow at 16 50.
Will he be on time? Explain your answer.

W You need Worksheet **9.4** for question **13**.

9.4 Timing

Example   The table shows the times for each contestant in a swimming race.

Name	Cherie	Claire	Barbara	Kylie	Frosini
Time (secs)	21·5	22·3	20·9	21·8	22·7

Who won the race?   The fastest swimmer has the lowest time.

Barbara won. Her time was 20·9 seconds.

Exercise 9.4

1 The 1500 metre race times for six boys are shown in the table.

Name	Phil	Tim	Dean	George	Drew	Alan
Time (mins)	5·2	5·8	6·1	5·3	6·7	5·9

(**a**) Who won the race?   (**b**) Who was second?   (**c**) Who was last?

2 Carole and John are racing their guinea pigs.
Whitey took 78·5 seconds and Blackie 69·8 seconds.
Which guinea pig won?

3 In a cycle time trial, pairs of cyclists compete against
each other.
For each pair, find the winner.

(**a**) Stan   23·55 seconds   (**b**) Fred   26·45 seconds   (**c**) Bill   23·35 seconds
     Alex   24·05 seconds   Pete   24·05 seconds   Greig   25·00 seconds

4 In the physics class, Mr Hill is recording pupil
reaction times.

(**a**) Who has the fastest time?

(**b**) Who has the slowest time?

Name	Time (secs)
Sara	1·25
Barry	0·85
Mona	0·99
Stella	1·10

5 On his car track, Brad and
his friends recorded the
times shown.

(**a**) Who had the fastest time?

(**b**) List the racers in order,
first to last.

(**c**) The average time for this
track is 15·83 seconds.
Which boys were faster
than the average?

Name	Lap time (secs)
Brad	15·85
Mel	14·05
Steve	16·75
Paul	14·95
Denzil	17·55

9.5 Calculating time intervals

Example   Claire's train leaves Edinburgh at 11 35 and arrives in Aberdeen
at 13 15. How long was the journey?

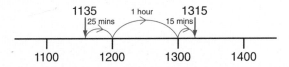

25 mins + 1 hour + 15 mins = 1 hour 40 mins

The journey took **1 hour 40 minutes**.

Exercise 9.5

1 Use the timetable to find the time to travel:
  (**a**) on bus A from Eaglesham to Govanhill
  (**b**) on bus C from Clarkston to Cathcart
  (**c**) on bus B from Muirend to Glasgow.

	Bus A	Bus B	Bus C
Eaglesham	09 00	10 15	11 30
Clarkston	09 12	10 28	11 42
Muirend	09 19	10 36	11 49
Cathcart	09 24	10 41	11 54
Govanhill	09 33	10 51	12 03
Gorbals	09 37	10 55	12 07
Glasgow	09 44	11 03	12 15

2 For each pair of start and finish times, calculate the journey time.

Journey	(a)	(b)	(c)	(d)	(e)	(f)
Start	08 15	09 40	10 35	13 55	17 40	19 20
Finish	09 25	10 55	11 54	15 45	19 05	22 00

3 Calculate the length of each TV programme.

Programme	Newsday	Westenders	Republic St	Showtime
Start time	17 30	19 25	20 00	21 20
Finish time	18 15	20 15	20 35	22 05

4 Four buses a day travel from Eaglesham to East Kilbride.
Use the timetable to calculate how long each bus takes.

	A	B	C	D
Eaglesham	07 35	11 35	15 45	18 10
East Kilbride	08 10	12 05	16 25	18 55

5 Use Michael's travel plan to calculate the time from:
  (**a**) Glasgow to Dover
  (**b**) Dover to Calais
  (**c**) Calais to St Omer
  (**d**) St Omer to Reims
  (**e**) Reims to Chalons.

Glasgow	6 a.m.
Dover	2.35 p.m.
Calais	4.35 p.m.
St Omer	7.45 p.m.
Reims	9.15 p.m.
Chalons	11.55 p.m.

6 Ian's working day starts at 08 30 and finishes at 17 15.
How long is his working day?

7 For a sponsored walk, Prue has to complete as many
laps as possible between 11.15 a.m. and 4 p.m.
How long will she be walking?

Review exercise 9

1 Write in words the time shown on each clock.

(**a**)   (**b**)   (**c**)

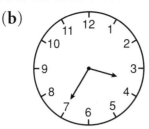

2 Write in words the time shown on each clock.

(**a**)   (**b**)   (**c**)

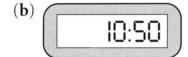
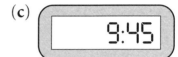

3 Write each time in figures using a.m. or p.m.:
(**a**) ten to six in the evening   (**b**) four thirty in the morning
(**c**) eight twenty at night   (**d**) noon.

4 Write each time in the twenty-four hour clock:
(**a**) 7 a.m.   (**b**) 12.20 p.m.   (**c**) 6.30 p.m.   (**d**) 2.15 a.m.

5 Copy and complete the table.

12-hour clock	2.25 p.m.					3.05 a.m.
24-hour clock		16 30	09 15	22 05	13 20	

6 Rupert has to deliver a letter before 5.30 p.m.
It will take him 35 minutes to deliver the letter.
His digital watch shows 16 45.
Does he still have time to make the delivery? Explain your answer.

7 The race times for three runners are shown in the table.
(**a**) Who has the fastest time?
(**b**) Who has the slowest time?

Sara	14·6 secs
Sakina	16·2 secs
Molly	15·9 secs

8 (**a**) Calculate the time taken for each lap in the cycle race.
(**b**) Which was the fastest lap?

Lap	1	2	3
Start time	13 15	13 25	13 45
Finish time	14 28	14 54	16 09

9 Stuart starts work at 7.15 a.m. and finishes at 2 p.m.
How long does he work?

Summary

24-hour clock

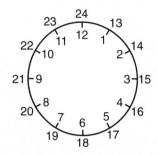

12-hour clock	24-hour clock
7.20 a.m.	07 20
10.05 p.m.	22 05

Use four figures for 24-hour clock.

For p.m. times, add 12 to the number of hours.

Timing

Which is the fastest time?

14·65 secs, 15·05 secs, 15·23 secs, 16·04 secs

  ↑   ↑

fastest time   slowest time

14·65 secs is the fastest time.

Calculating time intervals

Calculate the time interval from 08 55 to 13 20.

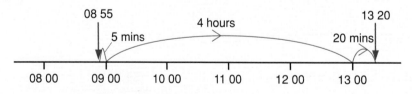

5 mins + 4 hours + 20 mins = 4 hours 25 mins

The time interval is **4 hours 25 minutes**.

10 Perimeter and area

In this chapter you will review perimeter and area. You will extend your knowledge to triangles and more complex shapes.

10.1 Perimeter

Remember
The **perimeter** of a shape is the total distance around the outside.
To find the perimeter of a shape **add** the lengths of **all** the sides.

Example 1
Find the perimeter of this rectangle.

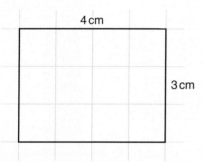

Perimeter = 4 + 3 + 4 + 3

Perimeter = **14 cm**

Example 2
Find the perimeter of this shape.

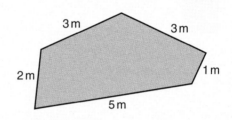

Perimeter = 2 + 3 + 3 + 1 + 5

Perimeter = **14 m**

Exercise 10.1

V You need Worksheet **10.1** for question **1**.

2 These shapes have been drawn on a grid of centimetre squares.
Find the perimeter of each shape.

(a)

(b)

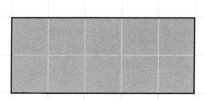

(c)

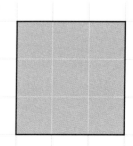

(**d**)   (**e**)   (**f**)

3 Find the perimeter of each shape.

(**a**)   (**b**)   (**c**)

(**d**)   (**e**)   (**f**)

(**g**)   (**h**)   (**i**)

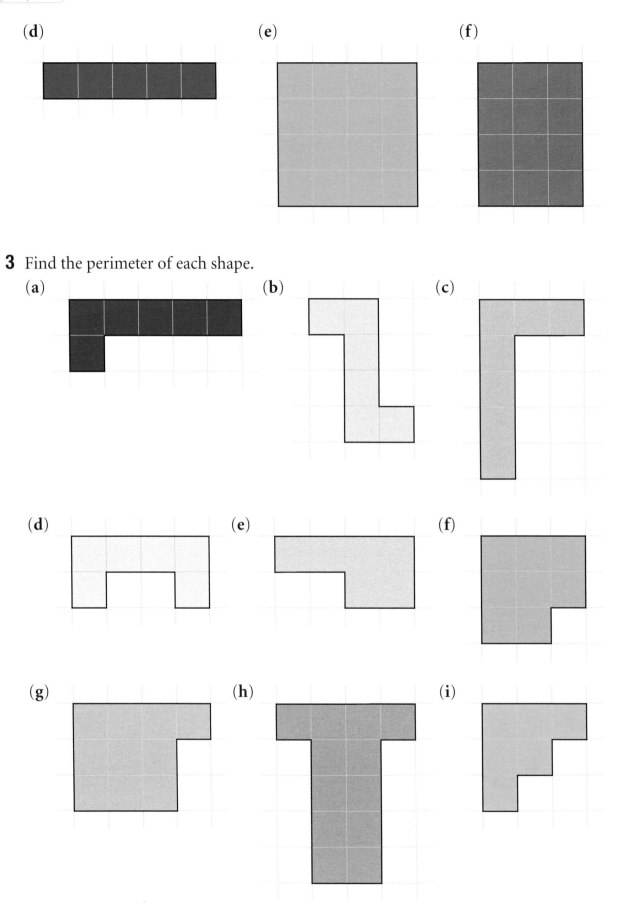

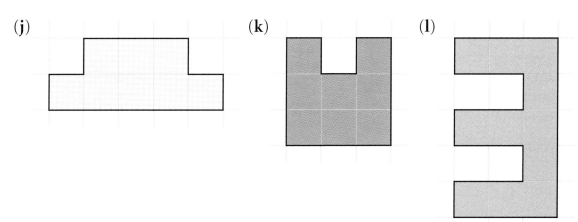

(j)   (k)   (l)

4 Calculate the perimeter of each shape.

(a) 5 cm, 3 cm, 4 cm

(b) 10 mm, 10 mm, 10 mm

(c) 2 m, 3 m, 4 m

(d) 3 cm, 3 cm, 2 cm

(e) 5 m, 2 m, 5 m, 2 m

(f) 3 cm, 3 cm, $2\frac{1}{2}$ cm, $2\frac{1}{2}$ cm

(g) 8 cm, 4 cm, 4 cm, 8 cm

(h) 5 m, 5 m, 4 m, 4 m, 7 m

(i) 6 cm, 6 cm, 5 cm, 5 cm, 6 cm, 6 cm

(j) $1\frac{1}{2}$ m, $1\frac{1}{2}$ m, $1\frac{1}{2}$ m, $1\frac{1}{2}$ m, $1\frac{1}{2}$ m, $1\frac{1}{2}$ m

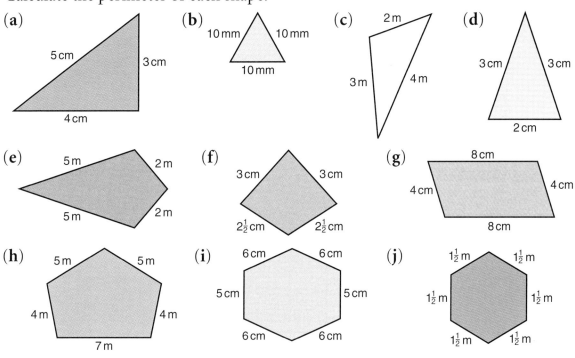

5 Farmer Brown plans to renew the fence round each of his three fields.

Bottom Meadow: 20 m, 35 m, 40 m, 45 m

High Park: 21 m, 25 m, 52 m, 35 m

Curlew Land: 20 m, 21 m, 25 m, 42 m, 33 m, 19 m

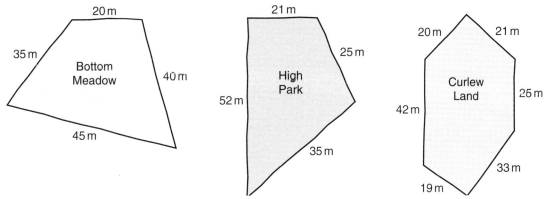

(a) Calculate the length of fence he will need for each field.

(b) Which field has the longest perimeter?

(c) If fencing costs £10 per metre, how much more does it cost to fence Bottom Meadow than High Park?

10.2 Area

Remember
The **area** of a shape is the amount of surface it covers.
Area can be measured in square centimetres.

1 square centimetre
(1 cm²)

The area of a rectangle = length × breadth

Example
Calculate the area of this rectangle.

Area = 5 × 4 = 20

Area of rectangle = 20 cm²

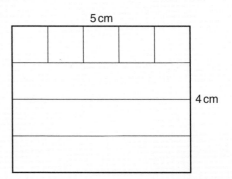

Exercise 10.2

W You need Worksheet **10.2** for question **1**.

2 Calculate the area of each rectangle.

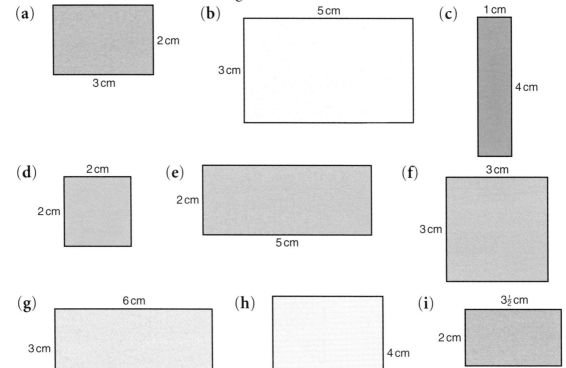

(a) 2 cm, 3 cm

(b) 5 cm, 3 cm

(c) 1 cm, 4 cm

(d) 2 cm, 2 cm

(e) 2 cm, 5 cm

(f) 3 cm, 3 cm

(g) 6 cm, 3 cm

(h) 4 cm, 4 cm

(i) 3½ cm, 2 cm

W You need Worksheet **10.3** for questions **3** and **4**.

10.3 Areas of more complex shapes

To calculate the area of a shape, count the number of complete squares and half squares.

Example

Find the area of this shape drawn on square dot paper.

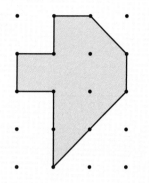

Area = 5 complete squares + 3 half squares

   = $5 + 1\frac{1}{2}$ squares

Total area $= 6\frac{1}{2}$ cm²

Exercise 10.3

1 These shapes have been drawn on square dot paper.
   Find the area of each shape.

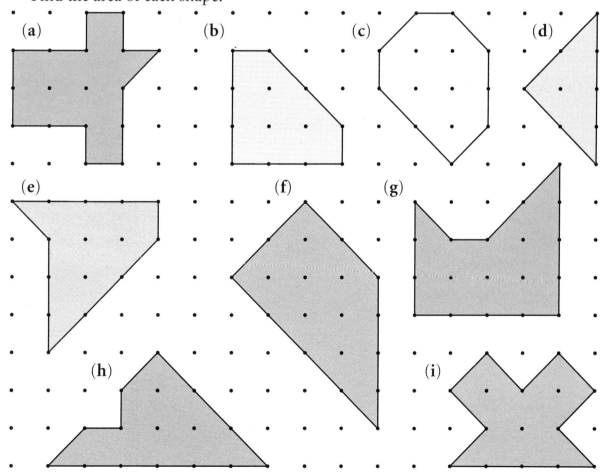

(a)

(b)

(c)

(d)

(e)

(f)

(g)

(h)

(i)

10.4 Area of a right-angled triangle

Example
Calculate the area of each shaded right-angled triangle.

(a)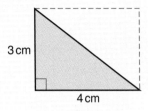

(b)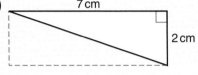

(c)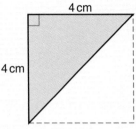

Area of rectangle
$$= 4 \times 3$$
$$= 12$$

Area of rectangle
$$= 2 \times 7$$
$$= 14$$

Area of square
$$= 4 \times 4$$
$$= 16$$

Area of shaded
triangle $= \frac{1}{2}$ of 12
$$= \mathbf{6\ cm^2}$$

Area of shaded
triangle $= \frac{1}{2}$ of 14
$$= \mathbf{7\ cm^2}$$

Area of shaded
triangle $= \frac{1}{2}$ of 16
$$= \mathbf{8\ cm^2}$$

Exercise 10.4

1 Calculate the area of each triangle.

(a)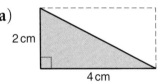

(b)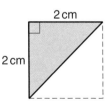

(c)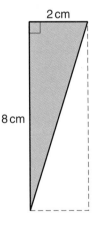

(d)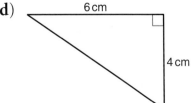

(e)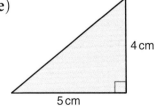

(f)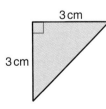

10.5 Area problems

Example
Calculate the areas of the shapes drawn
on the coordinate diagram.

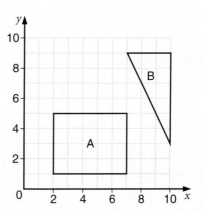

Area of rectangle A = 5 × 4

$\qquad$ = **20 square units**

Area of triangle B = $\frac{1}{2}$ of 3 × 6

$\qquad$ = $\frac{1}{2}$ of 18

$\qquad$ = **9 square units**

Exercise 10.5

1 Calculate the areas of these shapes:

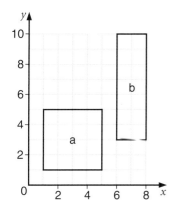 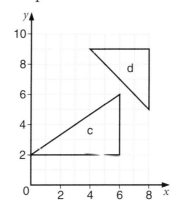 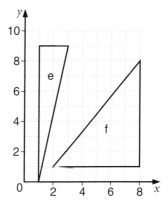

2 For each set of points, draw a coordinate diagram with axes from 0 to 10.
Plot the points, join them up and calculate the area of the shape.

(**a**) $(2, 1), (8, 1), (6, 6), (2, 6)$ 　　　　(**b**) $(3, 3), (8, 3), (8, 8), (3, 8)$

(**c**) $(0, 2), (10, 2), (10, 6)$ 　　　　　　(**d**) $(2, 3), (6, 3), (2, 9)$

(**e**) $(1, 9), (9, 9), (9, 1)$ 　　　　　　　(**f**) $(8, 0), (8, 9), (2, 9)$

3 Calculate the area of these pieces of carpet in the Grand Hotel.

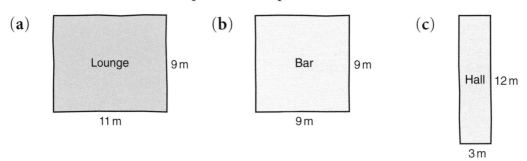

(a) Lounge — 9 m, 11 m

(b) Bar — 9 m, 9 m

(c) Hall — 12 m, 3 m

4 Ian is designing his new garden. He plans to have these sections. Calculate the area of each.

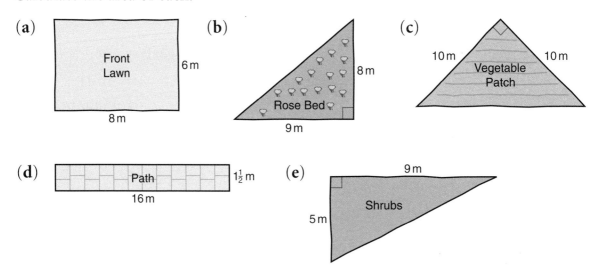

(a) Front Lawn — 6 m, 8 m

(b) Rose Bed — 8 m, 9 m

(c) Vegetable Patch — 10 m, 10 m

(d) Path — $1\frac{1}{2}$ m, 16 m

(e) Shrubs — 9 m, 5 m

5 Gary has decided to renew the wooden floors in parts of his house.

(a) Calculate the area of wood he will need for each room.

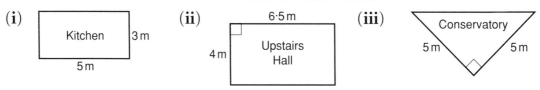

(i) Kitchen — 3 m, 5 m

(ii) Upstairs Hall — 6·5 m, 4 m

(iii) Conservatory — 5 m, 5 m

(b) Which floor will be most expensive to renew?

(c) What will it cost for the Upstairs Hall at £9 per square metre?

10.6 Areas of composite shapes

To find the area of a composite shape, calculate the area of each part and add them together.

Example
Calculate the area of this shape.

Area of rectangle A = 5 × 2   = 10

    Area of triangle B = $\frac{1}{2}$ of 4 × 3 =   6

                    Total area = 16 cm²

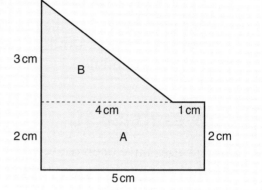

Exercise 10.6

You need Worksheet **10.4** for question **1**.

2 Calculate the total area of each shape.

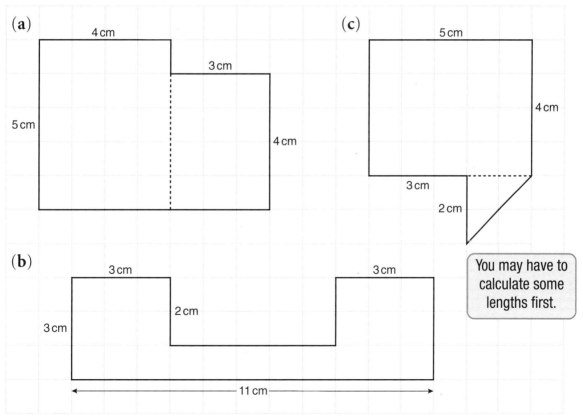

You may have to calculate some lengths first.

3 The diagram shows the plan of the ground floor of Carl's house.

(**a**) Calculate the area of each room.

(**b**) Calculate the total area of the ground floor.

(**c**) If the new carpet Carl likes costs £10 per square metre, what would it cost him to carpet all of the ground floor?

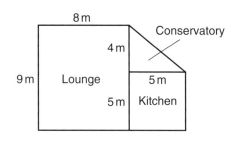

Review exercise 10

1 These shapes have been drawn on a grid of centimetre squares. Find the perimeter of each shape.

(**a**)   (**b**)   (**c**)

 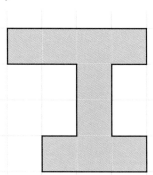 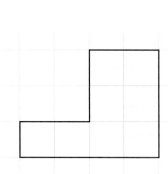

2 Calculate the perimeter of each shape in these sketches.

(**a**)   (**b**)   (**c**)

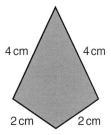 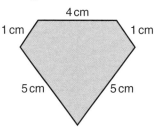 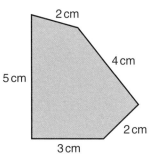

3 Calculate the area of each rectangle.

(**a**)   (**b**)   (**c**)

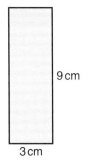 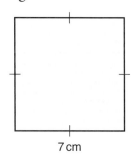 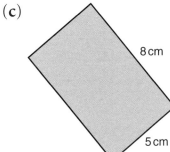

4 These shapes have been drawn on centimetre square dot paper.
Find the area of each shape.

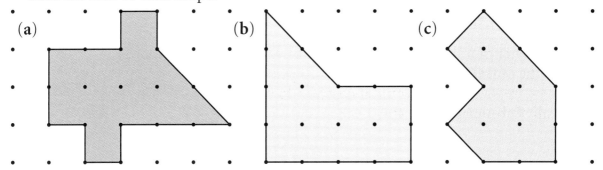

(a)   (b)   (c)

5 Calculate the area of each triangle.

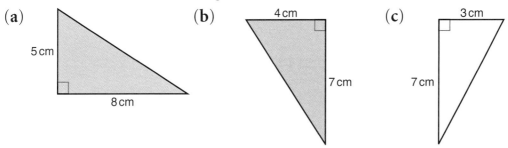

(a)   (b) 4 cm   (c) 3 cm

5 cm   7 cm   7 cm

8 cm

6 Draw a coordinate diagram with axes from 0 to 8.
  (a) Plot the points A(1, 2), B(7, 2) and C(7, 7).
  (b) Join the points to form triangle ABC.
  (c) Calculate the area of triangle ABC.

7 Joe cut the grass on the front lawn.
  (a) What area of grass did Joe cut?
  (b) Joe's dad paid him 10 pence per
      square metre.
      How much was Joe paid?

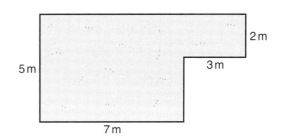

8 Calculate the total area of this shape.

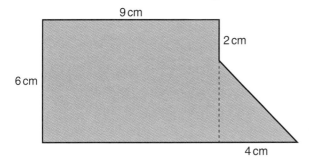

Summary

Perimeter

The perimeter of a shape is the total distance around the outside.

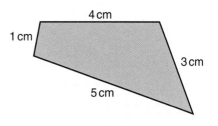

$$\text{Perimeter} = 1 + 4 + 3 + 5$$
$$= 13$$

Perimeter = 13 cm

Area

The area of a rectangle = length × breadth

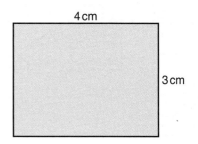

$$\text{Area} = 4 \times 3$$
$$= 12$$

Area = 12 cm²

Area of a right-angled triangle

The area of a right-angled triangle = $\frac{1}{2}$ (area of rectangle)

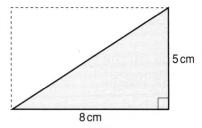

$$\text{Area} = \frac{1}{2} \text{ of } (8 \times 5)$$
$$= 20$$

Area = 20 cm²

Area of a composite shape

To find the area of a composite shape, add the area of each part.

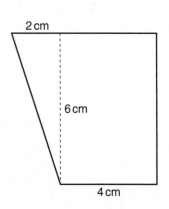

$$\text{Area of rectangle} = 6 \times 4 = 24$$
$$\text{Area of triangle} = \frac{1}{2} \text{ of } 2 \times 6 = 6$$

Total area = 30 cm²

11 Information handling

In this chapter you will review bar graphs and learn about line graphs, pie charts and scatter graphs.

11.1 Review

Remember
A bar graph displays information.

Example
From the bar graph:
(**a**) How many people chose chicken?
(**b**) Which was the most popular choice?

(**a**) **4** chose chicken. (**b**) **Fish** is the most popular.

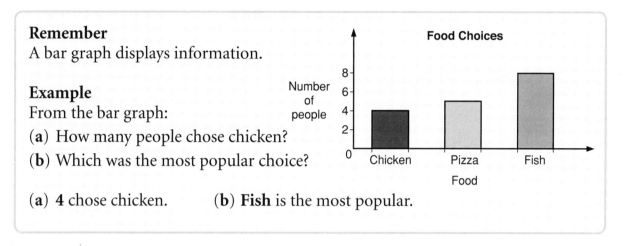

Exercise 11.1

1 (**a**) How many pupils in 2F2 have shoe size:
   (**i**) 3
   (**ii**) 4
   (**iii**) 6
   (**iv**) 7?
(**b**) Which is the most common shoe size?

2 Use the bar graph to answer the following.

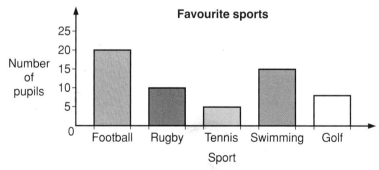

(**a**) Which is the most popular sport?
(**b**) Which is the least popular?
(**c**) How many people chose rugby?
(**d**) Which sport did 8 people choose?
(**e**) How many people were asked altogether?

3

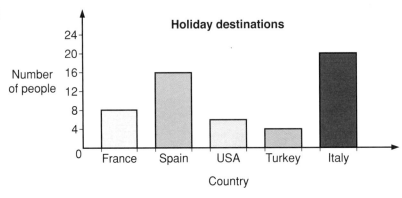

Holiday destinations

(**a**) Which is the most popular destination?

(**b**) How many went to Spain?

(**c**) Which is the least popular country?

(**d**) Which country did 6 people choose?

W You need Worksheet **11.1** for questions **4** to **7**.

8 Draw a bar graph to show the information in the table.

Favourite pasta	
Pasta	Number of people
Spaghetti	12
Tagliatelle	8
Penne	7
Macaroni	5
Fusilli	10
Lasagne	11

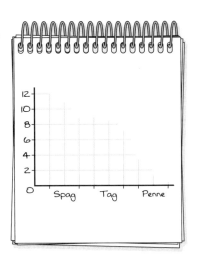

9 Draw a bar graph of the information in the table.

Number of boys in S2							
Class	2A	2B	2C	2D	2E	2F	2G
Number of boys	12	11	8	13	9	14	10

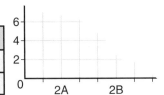

10 Draw a bar graph of the information in the table.

Career choice of pupils in 2A						
Choice	Nurse	Teacher	Doctor	Plumber	Dentist	Hairdresser
Number	4	6	3	8	2	5

11.2 Line graphs

Information may be displayed on a **line graph**.

Example
The line graph shows the temperature from 8 a.m. until 2 p.m.

(**a**) What was the temperature at 9 a.m.?

(**b**) What was the highest temperature and when did it occur?

(**a**) **3 °C**

(**b**) **9 °C** at **1 p.m.**

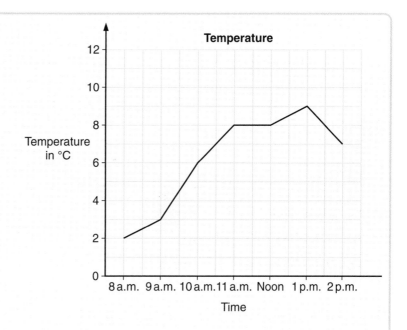

Exercise 11.2

1 Use the line graph above to answer the following.

(**a**) What was the temperature at 11 a.m.?

(**b**) At what time was the temperature 6 °C?

(**c**) What was the lowest temperature and when did it occur?

2 The enterprise club sells pens and pencils.

(**a**) How much profit did they make in May?

(**b**) In which month did they make £35 profit?

(**c**) Which was the most profitable month?

(**d**) Which was the least profitable month?

(**e**) How much did the profits rise from January to February?

(**f**) What happened to profits between March and April?

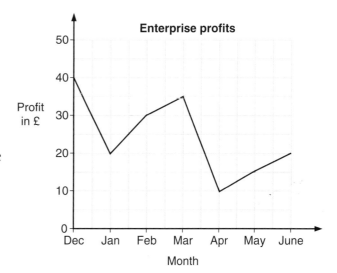

3 The office supervisor records telephone sales each week.

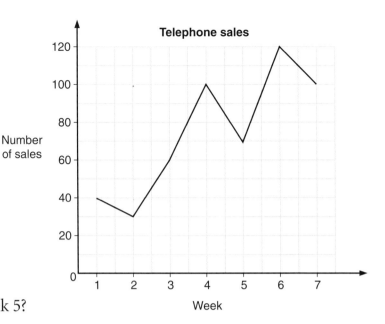

Telephone sales

(a) How many sales were there in week 3?

(b) In which week were sales at 100?

(c) In which week were sales highest?

(d) What was the rise in sales from week 2 to week 3?

(e) What was the drop in sales from week 4 to week 5?

W You need Worksheet **11.2** for questions **4** to **7**.

8 Draw a line graph to show the information on Redburn Rovers' league results.

Annual results						
Year	2000	2001	2002	2003	2004	2005
Points	30	25	15	40	35	30

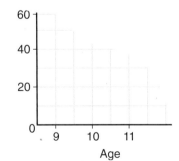

(a) Which year was their best?

(b) Between which years did they have the biggest drop?

(c) If they score over 35 points, the players are paid a bonus. In which years did they earn the bonus?

9 Natalie records her daughter's height on her birthday every year.
Draw a line graph to show her information.

Annual height								
Age	9	10	11	12	13	14	15	16
Height (cm)	130	131	133	138	144	146	147	147

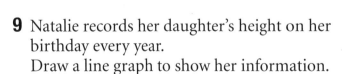

(a) Between which two ages did she grow the most?

(b) Natalie thinks her daughter will grow to be over 150 centimetres. Do you think she will be? Explain your answer.

10 At a fish research station, the maximum height of a river is recorded each year.
Draw a line graph to show the information.

Maximum river height							
Year	1999	2000	2001	2002	2003	2004	2005
Height (m)	2·2	2·5	1·8	1·6	2·9	2·6	2·7

(**a**) Which year was the river at its highest?

(**b**) When the river is over 2·6 metres high, the research station floods.
In which years did it flood?

(**c**) Are floods becoming more or less common?

11.3 Pie charts

A **pie chart** displays information.

| The smallest sector shows the least popular choice. |

Favourite programmes

Example
From the pie chart, write the programmes
in order of popularity, from most to least
popular.

| The largest sector shows the most popular choice. |

Soaps, films, comedies, sport, music.

Exercise 11.3

1 From the pie chart:

(**a**) Which is the most common pet?

(**b**) Which is the least common pet?

(**c**) Do more people own cats than goldfish?

(**d**) 'Budgies are more popular than cats.'
True or false?

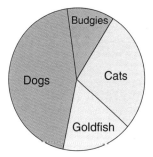

Pet ownership

2 From the pie chart:

(**a**) Which is the most popular holiday destination?

(**b**) Colin says the USA is more popular than Italy.
Is he correct?

(**c**) Write the destinations in order of popularity,
from most to least popular.

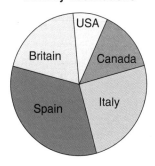

Holiday destinations

3 The pie chart shows the revision time Ruth spends on each subject.

(**a**) Which subject has the same time as English?

(**b**) List the subjects with the same time as History.

(**c**) List the subjects with the same time as IT.

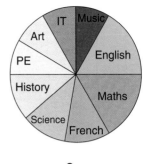

Subject time

4 People were asked to name their major concerns. The results are displayed in the pie chart.

(**a**) What causes most concern?

(**b**) What is of least concern?

(**c**) List the concerns in order, from least to most.

Concerns

W You need Worksheet **11.3** for questions **5** to **8**.

9 From the pie chart, list pasta choices in order of popularity, from least to most popular.

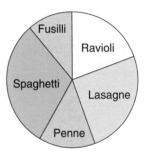

Pasta choices

11.4 Scatter graphs

A **scatter graph** displays the connection between two sets of information.

Example

(**a**) Find the height and weight of:
   (**i**) Sue   (**ii**) Pam.

(**b**) Are taller people heavier?

(**a**) (**i**) Sue is **125 cm** tall and weighs **54 kg**.
   (**ii**) Pam is **130 cm** tall and weighs **58 kg**.

(**b**) **Yes.** In general, taller people are heavier.

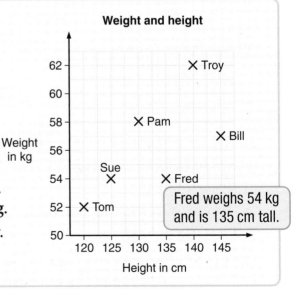

Weight and height

Fred weighs 54 kg and is 135 cm tall.

Exercise 11.4

1 From the scatter graph, write the height and weight of:

(**a**) Tina

(**b**) Prue

(**c**) Abby

(**d**) May

(**e**) Gerry.

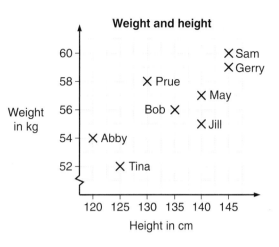

2 From the scatter graph:

(**a**) How old is Joe?

(**b**) What is Pete's shoe size?

(**c**) What is the shoe size of the 9-year-old child?

(**d**) What age is the person with size 39 shoes?

(**e**) Do older people have bigger feet? Explain your answer.

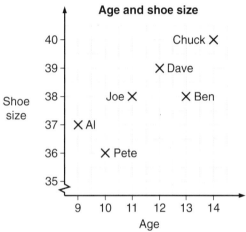

3 From the scatter graph:

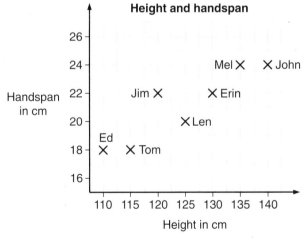

(**a**) How tall is Jim?

(**b**) What is Tom's handspan?

(**c**) Who is tallest?

(**d**) How tall is the person with the 20 centimetre handspan?

(**e**) What is the handspan of the person who is 140 centimetres tall?

(**f**) Do taller people have a greater handspan? Explain your answer.

(**g**) How many people were measured for this graph?

4 From the scatter graph:

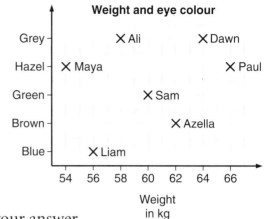

Weight and eye colour

(**a**) How heavy is Ali?

(**b**) What colour are Paul's eyes?

(**c**) What is Maya's weight?

(**d**) Who has green eyes?

(**e**) How heavy is the person with brown eyes?

(**f**) What colour are the eyes of the person who weighs 56 kg?

(**g**) Is eye colour related to weight? Explain your answer.

W You need Worksheet **11.4** for questions **5** to **8**.

Review exercise 11

1 From the bar graph:

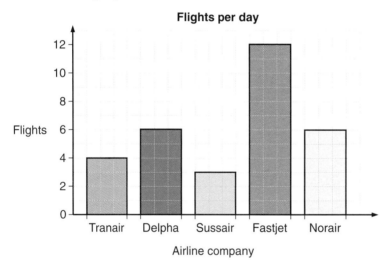

Flights per day

(**a**) How many Tranair flights are there each day?

(**b**) Which company has three flights each day?

(**c**) Which two airlines have the same number of flights each day?

(**d**) Which airline has the most flights per day?

(**e**) How many more flights per day has Fastjet than Tranair?

2 Use the information in the table to draw a bar graph.

Fastran delivery service					
Day	Mon	Tues	Wed	Thurs	Fri
Parcels delivered	8	12	11	9	7

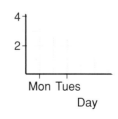

3 From the line graph:

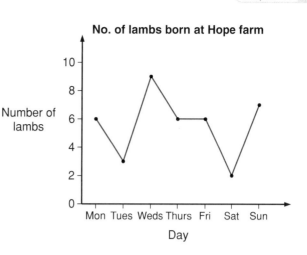

No. of lambs born at Hope farm

(**a**) How many lambs were born on Tuesday?

(**b**) On which day were most lambs born?

(**c**) How many more lambs were born on Sunday than Saturday?

(**d**) How many lambs were born after Thursday?

4 Use the information below to draw a line graph.

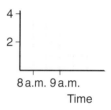

Temperature						
Time	8 a.m.	9 a.m.	10 a.m.	11 a.m.	Noon	1 p.m.
Temp °C	1	3	6	7	8	5

5 The pie chart shows the food choices in the school dining hall.
List the choices in order, from least to most popular.

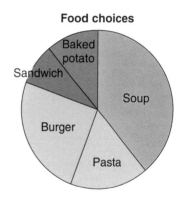

Food choices

6 From the scatter graph:

(**a**) How old is Phil?

(**b**) What music grade has Maria passed?

(**c**) Who is at grade 6?

(**d**) How old is the person at grade 3?

(**e**) What grade has the 16-year-old achieved?

(**f**) Do older pupils pass higher grades? Explain your answer.

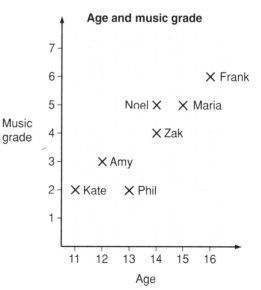

Age and music grade

Summary

Bar graphs

Information may be shown on a bar graph.

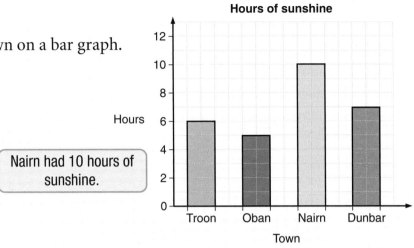

Nairn had 10 hours of sunshine.

Line graphs

Information may be shown on a line graph.

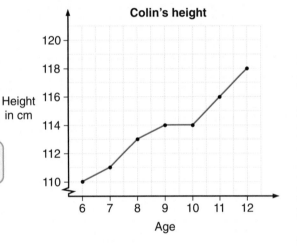

Colin was 116 cm at age 11.

Pie charts

Information may be shown on a pie chart.

Most pupils travel to school by bus.

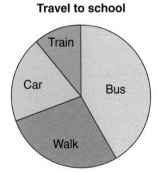

Scatter graphs

A scatter graph displays the connection between two sets of information.

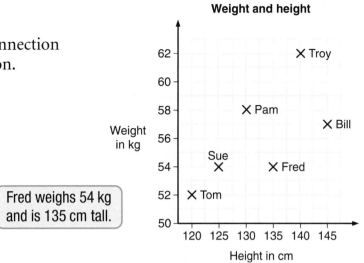

Weight and height

Fred weighs 54 kg and is 135 cm tall.

12 Number patterns and formulae

In this chapter you will revise and extend your knowledge of sequences.
You will also learn to construct word formulae.

12.1 Sequences

Remember

A sequence is a list of numbers that are in a particular order.

2, 4, 6, 8, 10, 12, 14…	is a sequence of even numbers.
5, 10, 15, 20, 25, 30…	is a sequence that goes up in fives.
19, 17, 15, 13, 11, 9…	is a sequence that goes down in twos.

A rule can be written to continue a sequence.

Sequence	Rule
1, 3, 5, 7, 9, 11……	Add 2 to find the next number.
30, 27, 24, 21, 18…	Subtract 3 to find the next number.

Exercise 12.1

W You need Worksheet **12.1** for question **1**.

2 For each of these starting numbers and rules, write the first six numbers in the sequence.

	Start number	Rule for the next number
(**a**)	50	Add 1
(**b**)	40	Subtract 4
(**c**)	0	Add 9
(**d**)	100	Subtract 10
(**e**)	100	Add 100
(**f**)	$5\frac{1}{2}$	Subtract $\frac{1}{2}$
(**g**)	12·5	Subtract 2

50, 51, 52…

40, 36, 32…

3 Our house is the first in the street and is number one.
The house numbers increase by 2 on our side of
the street.
Write the sequence of house numbers for the
ten houses on our side of the street.

4 Each time Tesfa washes his Dad's car he is given double the
amount he was given the time before. He is given £1 the first
time, £2 the second time, £4 the third time and so on.
How much will he be given the seventh time he washes the car?

5 (**a**) Write the first twelve numbers in each of these sequences:
    (**i**) 120, 110, 100…   (**ii**) 1, 4, 7, 10…
(**b**) Write any numbers that appear in both sequences.

6 For each of these sequences, draw the next two
diagrams and find the next two numbers:

(**a**) Triangular numbers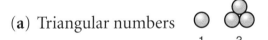

(**b**) Rectangular numbers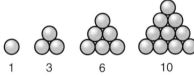

(**c**) Square numbers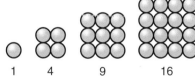

7 In these sequences the first two numbers add to give the third.
Each number after that is the sum of the two before it.
Find the next two numbers in each sequence:

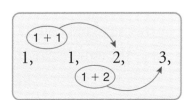

(**a**) 1, 1, 2, 3, 5, 8……
(**b**) 1, 3, 4, 7, 11……
(**c**) 3, 5, 8, 13, 21……

12.2 Constructing formulae in words

Legs on horses

The next pattern in the sequence would be:

The number of horses and legs can be shown in a table.

Number of horses	Number of legs
1	4
2	8
3	12
4	16

The number of legs increases 4 at a time.

The number of legs is 4 times the number of horses. You can use this formula to find the number of legs when you know the number of horses.

For 6 horses there would be 4 × 6 = **24 legs**.

For 20 horses there would be 4 × 20 = **80 legs**.

Exercise 12.2

W You need Worksheets **12.2** and **12.3** for questions **1** to **4**.

5 Men in a boat

(**a**) Draw the next pattern in the sequence.

(**b**) Copy and complete the table.

(**c**) Find the increase in the number of men each time.

(**d**) Copy and complete the formula:

The number of men is ……… times the number of boats.

(**e**) Use your formula to find how many men are in:

    (**i**) 5 boats   (**ii**) 9 boats.

Number of boats	Number of men
1	3
2	
3	
4	

12.3 Formulae from matchstick patterns

Exercise 12.3

Shape no.	No. of matches

W You need Worksheets **12.4** and **12.5** for questions **1** to **4**.

5 For each sequence of matchstick shapes:
- Draw the next pattern in the sequence.
- Make a table.
- Find the increase in the number of matches each time.
- Write a formula that starts:

  The number of matches is ......

- Use the formula to find the number of matches in the 10th pattern.

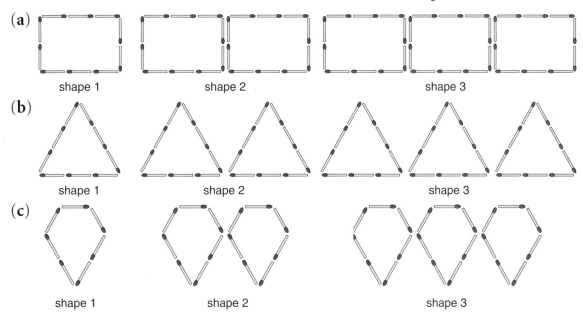

(a) shape 1   shape 2   shape 3

(b) shape 1   shape 2   shape 3

(c) shape 1   shape 2   shape 3

Review exercise 12

1 For each of these starting numbers and rules, write the first six numbers in the sequence.
(**a**) Start with 3. Add 5 for the next number.
(**b**) Start with 40. Subtract 4 for the next number.
(**c**) Start with 1. Multiply by 2 for the next number.
(**d**) Start with $\frac{1}{2}$. Add $\frac{1}{2}$ for the next number.

2 Continue each sequence for the next three numbers.
(**a**) 1, 8, 15, 22…   (**b**) 99, 96, 93, 90…
(**c**) 10, 21, 32, 43…   (**d**) 42, 46, 50, 54…

3 One Saturday morning Ben has £41.
Each day for the next week he spends £5.

(**a**) Write a sequence for the amount of money Ben has each evening for that week.

(**b**) How much does Ben still have to spend next Saturday morning?

4 Eggs in a box

(**a**) Draw the next pattern in the sequence.

(**b**) Copy and complete the table.

(**c**) Find the increase in the number of eggs each time.

(**d**) Copy and complete the formula:

*The number of eggs is .... times
the number of boxes.*

(**e**) Use your formula to find how many eggs are in:

(**i**) 7 boxes   (**ii**) 10 boxes.

Number of boxes	Number of eggs
1	
2	
3	
4	

5 For this pattern of shapes made from matchsticks:

- Draw the next pattern in the sequence.
- Make a table showing **Number of shapes** and **Number of matches**.
- Find the increase in the number of matches each time.
- Write a formula that starts:

The number of matches is ......

- Use the formula to find the number of matches in the 7th pattern.

shape 1   shape 2   shape 3

Summary

Sequence

A sequence is a list of numbers in a particular order.

Sequence	Rule
2, 6, 10, 14, 18…	Add 4 for the next number.

Constructing formulae

- Understand the pattern by reading the word explanation and drawing the next picture.

Plants in a pot

- Draw a table to show the pattern of numbers.

Number of pots	Number of plants
1	4
2	8
3	12
4	16

- Find the increase.   The number of plants increases by 4 each time.
- Write the formula.   The number of plants is 4 × the number of pots.

13 2D shape

In this chapter you will learn more about two-dimensional shapes, including the circle.

13.1 Units of length

We use different units for measuring lengths.

Object				
Unit	millimetre	centimetre	metre	kilometre

For drawing and measuring shapes on paper, we use millimetres and centimetres.

Example 1
Measure the length of side PQ in the triangle.

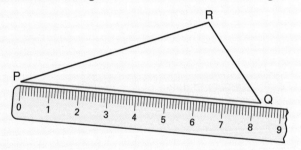

PQ is **8·3 cm** long.

8·3 cm may be written
as 8 cm 3 mm

Example 2
Draw a rectangle with dimensions: length 6 cm, breadth 2·8 cm

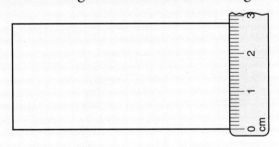

Exercise 13.1

1 Which units would you use to measure the length of a:
  (**a**) pin   (**b**) room   (**c**) book   (**d**) river   (**e**) pen
  (**f**) table   (**g**) street   (**h**) nail   (**i**) sleeve   (**j**) journey?

W You need Worksheet **13.1** for questions **2** to **4**.

5 (**a**) Draw rectangles with the dimensions shown.

Rectangle	Length	Breadth
W	4 cm	5 cm
X	3·5 cm	6·2 cm
Y	5·8 cm	5·8 cm
Z	8·3 cm	2·9 cm

(**b**) What is special about rectangle Y?

6 The diagrams show sketches of house plans.
Draw each one accurately using the measurements shown.

(**a**)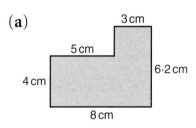

(**b**)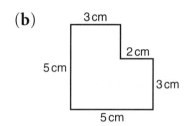

(**c**)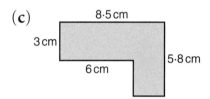

13.2 Triangles

Remember

A **right-angled** triangle has

 1 right angle

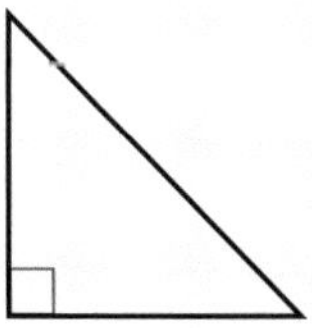

An **equilateral** triangle has

 3 equal sides

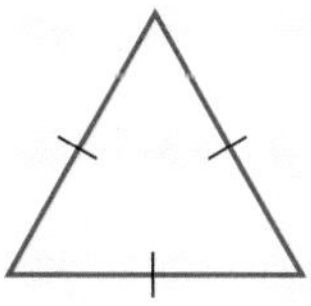

An **isosceles** triangle has

 2 equal sides

A **scalene** triangle has

 3 sides of different length

Exercise 13.2

1 Name each type of triangle.

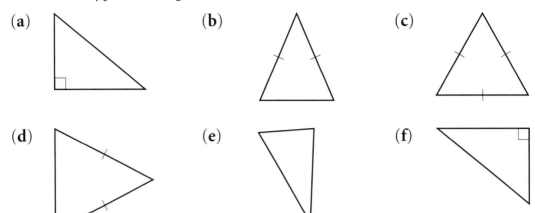

(a) (b) (c)

(d) (e) (f)

W You need Worksheet **13.2** for question **2**.

3 Draw:
  (**a**) a right-angled triangle with shorter sides of length 5 cm and 6·4 cm
  (**b**) an isosceles triangle with two sides of 7·4 cm.

13.3 Terminology

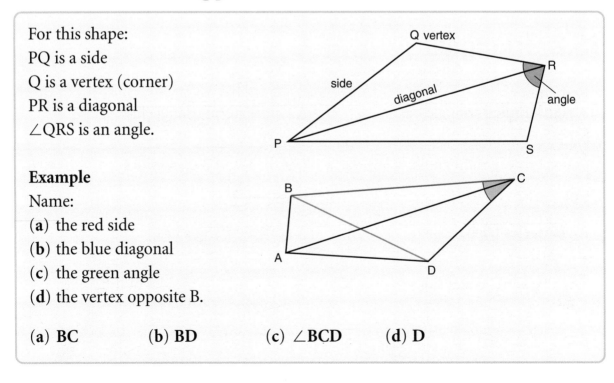

For this shape:
PQ is a side
Q is a vertex (corner)
PR is a diagonal
∠QRS is an angle.

Example
Name:
  (**a**) the red side
  (**b**) the blue diagonal
  (**c**) the green angle
  (**d**) the vertex opposite B.

(**a**) **BC**   (**b**) **BD**   (**c**) ∠**BCD**   (**d**) **D**

Exercise 13.3

W You need Worksheet **13.3** for questions **1** and **2**.

3 For each diagram, name the red side, red diagonal and red angle.

(**a**)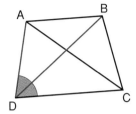

(**b**)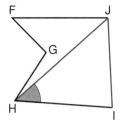

(**c**)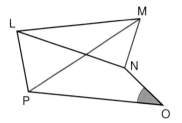

4 For each diagram, name the green side, green diagonal and green angle.

(**a**)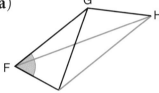

(**b**)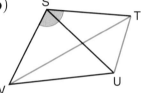

(**c**)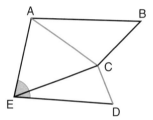

5 (**a**) Sketch a rectangle with vertices A, B, C and D.

(**b**) Draw in the diagonals.

13.4 Pentagons and hexagons

A pentagon has five sides.   A hexagon has six sides.

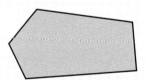   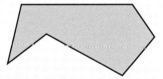

A regular shape has all sides and angles the same size.

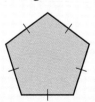

Regular pentagon   Regular hexagon

Exercise 13.4

1 Name each shape. | Triangle, square, rectangle, pentagon, hexagon |

(a)   (b)   (c)   (d)

(e)   (f)   (g)   (h)

(i)   (j)   (k)   (l)

2 (a) Sketch a pentagon.
   (b) Draw in all the diagonals.
   (c) How many diagonals has a pentagon?

3 (a) Sketch a hexagon.
   (b) Draw in all the diagonals.
   (c) How many diagonals has a hexagon?

W You need Worksheet **13.4** for question **4**.

13.5 The circle

A circle is a 2D shape in which all points on the edge are the same distance from the centre.

The distance round a circle is called the **circumference**.

The distance from the **centre** to the circumference is called the **radius**.

The distance across the circle, through the centre, is called the **diameter**.

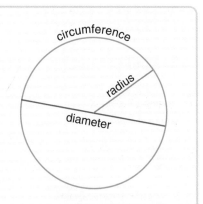

Exercise 13.5

W You need Worksheet **13.5** for questions **1** and **2**.

3 For each circle, write the length of the diameter.

(a) 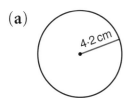   (b) 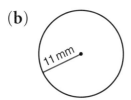   (c) 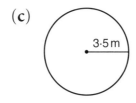   (d)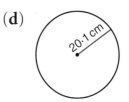

4 For each circle, write the length of the radius.

(a) 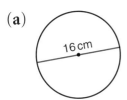   (b) 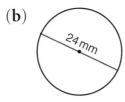   (c) 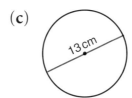   (d)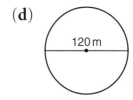

5 Copy and complete the table for circles.

Length of radius	4 cm	9 cm			12 m	25 km	
Length of diameter			22 m	9 cm			62 km

6 Copy and complete the table for each circle.

(a)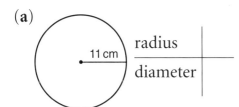

radius |
---|---
diameter |

(b)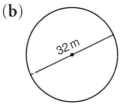

radius |
---|---
diameter |

7 Find the distance from P to Q in each diagram.

(a) 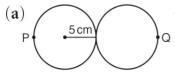   (b)    (c)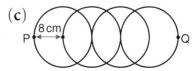

13.6 Drawing circles

In ancient times, to mark a circle on the ground,
a rope was tied to a pole.

On paper, we use a set of compasses to draw a circle.

Example

Draw a circle of radius 5 centimetres.

Set the compasses to 5 centimetres against a ruler.

Place the point of the compasses on the paper and
carefully rotate the pencil around the point.

Exercise 13.6

1 Draw a circle with radius:
   (**a**) 5 cm   (**b**) 7 cm   (**c**) 6·5 cm

2 Draw a circle with diameter 12 cm.

> Find the radius first.

3 Draw semicircles of radius:
   (**a**) 4 cm   (**b**) 10 cm

> A semicircle is a half circle.

W You need Worksheet **13.6** for question **4**.

Review exercise 13

You need compasses for question **9**.

1 Which unit of length would you use to measure:
   (**a**) a desk   (**b**) a pin
   (**c**) a carpet   (**d**) the length of a lake?

> millimetre   centimetre
> metre   kilometre

2 Measure the length of each line.
   (**a**) _____   (**b**) _____

3 Measure the length and width of this rectangle.

4 Draw accurately:

(**a**) a rectangle 8·5 centimetres long and 6 centimetres broad

(**b**) a square of side 4·6 cm.

5 Name each type of triangle:

(**a**) 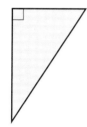   (**b**) 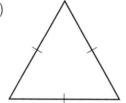   (**c**)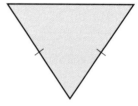

6 For this shape name:

(**a**) the diagonal

(**b**) the red side

(**c**) the blue angle.

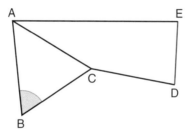

7 (**a**) Which shape is a pentagon?

(**b**) Which shape is a hexagon?

 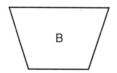   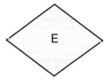

8 For this circle, what colour is:

(**a**) the circumference

(**b**) the radius

(**c**) the diameter?

9 Draw a circle of radius 5·5 centimetres.

Summary

Units of length

We use the units   millimetre (mm)
centimetre (cm)
metre (m)
kilometre (km)   to measure length.

Triangles

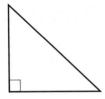  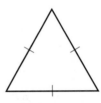 

Right-angled   Isosceles   Equilateral   Scalene

Terminology

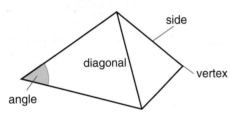

Pentagons and hexagons

   5 sides   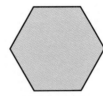   6 sides

Pentagon   Hexagon

Circles

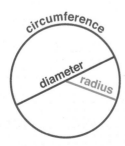

Diameter is double the radius.

14 Information handling 2

In this chapter you will review how to organise and display information and learn about averages.

14.1 Frequency tables

After data has been collected, it is useful to organise it in a table.
A frequency table shows you how often each piece of data occurs.

These are Steven's scores from a round of golf.

4 4 3 4 5 3 3 4 4

3 2 4 3 5 3 4 5 4

Organise these scores in a frequency table.

The lowest score is 2.
The highest score is 5.

Score	Tally	Frequency
2			1
3								6
4										8
5						3

The **mode**, or most frequent score, is **4**.

Exercise 14.1

You need Worksheet **14.1** for question **1**.

2 You need Worksheet **14.2** for this question.
For each set of data:
- complete the frequency table
- write the mode.

(a) Colour of hair:

Blonde	Black	Brown	Red	Blonde	Brown	Blonde	Brown
Brown	Black	Blonde	Black	Brown	Red	Blonde	Black
Brown	Brown	Blonde	Black	Brown	Black	Blonde	Brown
Black	Brown	Red	Black	Black	Brown	Red	Brown
Black	Brown	Red	Brown	Black	Brown	Red	Brown

(**b**) Colour of eyes:

Blue	Green	Brown	Blue	Blue	Brown	Blue	Brown
Brown	Blue	Green	Blue	Brown	Blue	Blue	Blue
Brown	Brown	Blue	Green	Brown	Blue	Blue	Brown
Hazel	Blue	Blue	Green	Blue	Brown	Green	Blue
Hazel	Brown	Green	Brown	Blue	Brown	Brown	Brown

(**c**) Goals scored each game by school football team:

4 6 1 5 2   0 5 3 2 4
1 2 1 4 2   2 2 0 4 3

(**d**) Shoe size of second year girls:

3 6 5 4 3   6 5 3 5 4
5 7 5 4 5   6 3 6 4 5
6 6 7 5 5   5 5 3 7 4
7 5 5 4 6   3 6 5 4 6

3 (**a**) Make your own frequency table to show each of these golf scores.

Stella:

4 3 3 5 5 4 4 4 5
3 3 5 3 5 3 4 6 4

Gwen:

5 4 3 5 6 4 5 5 5
4 2 5 4 6 4 6 7 5

Dana:

6 5 4 6 6 4 5 5 5
4 4 6 4 7 4 6 7 5

(**b**) For each person, write the mode.

4 The following gives the number of goals scored by Scottish football teams one Saturday.

Aberdeen	2	Dundee	1	St. Mirren	2	Falkirk	6
Dundee United	1	Dunfermline	2	Clyde	2	St Johnstone	2
Hibernian	2	Hearts	2	Airdrie Utd	1	Queen of the South	2
Inverness CT	2	Celtic	1	Ross County	5	Partick Thistle	1
Motherwell	3	Kilmarnock	1	Hamilton Ac.	3	Raith Rovers	0
Rangers	4	Livingston	0				

(**a**) Construct a frequency table to show the number of goals scored.

(**b**) What was the modal number of goals scored?

> The modal number is another way of saying the **mode**.

14.2 Displaying information.

When data has been organised, it is useful to display it on a graph.

Example
The frequency table shows the colours
of cars passing a busy junction.

Draw a bar graph to
show this information.

A bar graph must have:

- bars of equal width
- axes clearly marked
- axes clearly labelled
- a title.

Colour	Tally	Frequency
Red	||||| ||||| ||||| |||	18
Blue	||||| ||||| |||	13
Green	||||| |||||	10
White	||||| |||	8
Black	|||||		6
Silver	|||	3

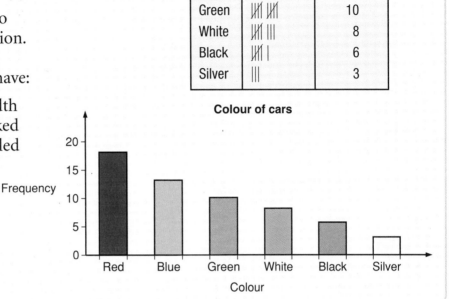

Colour of cars

Exercise 14.2

You need Worksheet **14.3** for question **1**.

2 Construct a bar graph to display the information in each frequency table.

(**a**) Favourite football team

Club	Frequency
Ross County	12
Alloa	10
Gretna	4
Elgin City	6
Morton	12

(**b**) Urban bird survey

Bird	Frequency
Seagull	20
Starling	10
Sparrow	15
Magpie	5
Blackbird	15

(**c**) Favourite pop group

Group	Frequency
Dizoninz	20
Tuned Out	10
Flat by Miles	15
Broken Kord	5
Screamin' Bairns	15

(**d**) Family size

No. of children	Frequency
1	8
2	12
3	6
4	3
5	1

3 For each set of data:
- construct a frequency table
- draw a bar graph of the information.

(**a**) Colour of hair:

Brown	Black	Red	Black
Black	Black	Red	Brown
Brown	Brown	Blonde	Blonde
Blonde	Black	Blonde	Red
Black	Brown	Red	Black
Brown	Red	Brown	Black
Black	Brown	Red	Brown
Black	Black	Blonde	Brown
Blonde	Brown	Blonde	Brown
Black	Brown	Blonde	Brown

(**b**) Goals scored by school hockey team:

4	2	0	4	0		2	2	1	3	3
4	2	3	5	2		0	1	3	2	2

(**c**) Shoe size of second year boys:

6	6	10	9	6		6	7	9	6	8
9	8	5	10	5		7	6	6	8	5
6	6	7	6	5		5	5	9	7	7
7	8	7	9	6		6	6	5	7	6

W You need Worksheet **14.4** for questions **4** and **5**.

14.3 Interpreting bar graphs

Sometimes it is useful to construct a frequency table from a bar graph.

A group of pupils was surveyed to find their favourite bird of prey.
Use rhe bar graph to complete the frequency table.

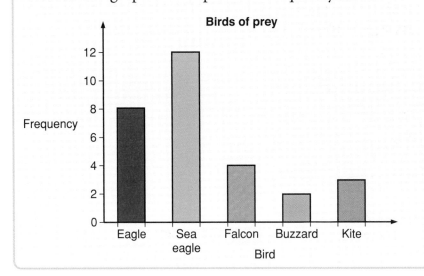

Bird	Frequency
Eagle	8
Sea eagle	12
Falcon	4
Buzzard	2
Kite	3

Exercise 14.3

N You need Worksheet **14.5** for question **1**.

2 Construct a frequency table for each bar graph.

(a)

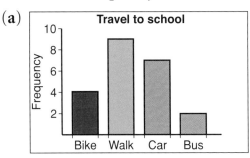

(b)

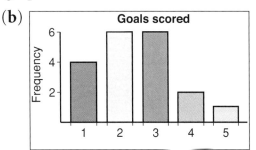

(c)

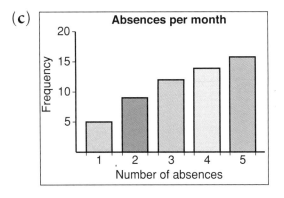

(d)

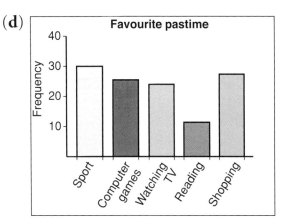

14.4 The mean

The **mean** is a type of average.

To find the mean:
- calculate the total
- divide the total by the number of pieces of data.

Example

This data shows the number of otters spotted each day at a nature reserve.

$$5 \quad 6 \quad 8 \quad 0 \quad 1 \longleftarrow$$

Find the mean number of otters per day.

5 pieces of data.

Total $= 5 + 6 + 8 + 0 + 1 = 20$

Mean $= 20 \div 5 = 4$

The mean number of otters per day is **4**.

Exercise 14.4

1 Find the mean for each set of data.

(**a**) 4 8 7 5 6   (**b**) 2 7 3 4 5 3

(**c**) 8 4 5 7   (**d**) 9 3 6 9 8

(**e**) 5 5 6 5 4   (**f**) 3 5 6 2 2 6

(**g**) 3 8 6 5 4 6 3   (**h**) 9 5 8 2 2 8 6 9 3 4

2 This data shows a golfer's scores for the first 10 holes of golf for 2 different days.

Round 1
3 7 5 6 3
6 5 4 7 3

Round 2
6 7 4 3 6
5 4 7 3 2

(**a**) Calculate the mean score for each day.

(**b**) Which day had the lowest mean?

3 This data shows the number of seagulls spotted on 5 days for two different towns.

(**a**) Calculate the mean number of seagulls for each town.

Waytown
35 17 25 16 27

Erskine
36 27 14 63 46

(**b**) Which town had the highest mean?

(**c**) Which town is at the seaside? Explain your answer.

Review exercise 14

1 For each set of data:
- construct a frequency table
- draw a bar graph of the information.

(**a**) Favourite colour:

Black	Red	Yellow	Green	Pink	Pink	Green	Purple
Black	Yellow	Green	Red	Blue	Purple	Red	Black
Pink	Green	Black	Blue	Red	Purple	Blue	Yellow
Brown	Purple	Blue	Green	Purple	Yellow	Blue	Pink
Yellow	Blue	Green	Blue	Black	Blue	Red	Blue

(**b**) Number of brothers and sisters:

2 3 1 5 2   0 5 3 2 1
1 4 2 4 1   3 4 2 1 1
2 2 0 1 4   0 1 2 2 2

2 Construct a frequency table for each bar graph.

(**a**)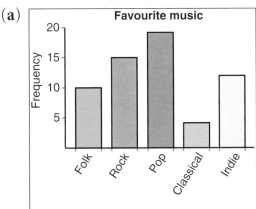

(**b**)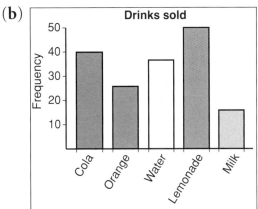

3 Find the mean score for each of these sets of data:

(**a**) 5 6 8 7 4   (**b**) 8 6 2 0 3 5
(**c**) 7 1 7 9   (**d**) 6 9 9 8 8

4 This data shows the number of goals scored in ten games by two school football teams.

First year
6 2 8 6 1
3 7 0 4 3

Second year
3 0 2 4 2
6 3 5 3 2

(**a**) Calculate the mean score for each team.
(**b**) Which team had the highest mean?

Summary

Frequency tables

It is useful to organise data in a frequency table.

4	4	3	4	5	3	3	4	4
3	2	4	3	5	3	4	5	4

Score	Tally	Frequency
2			1
3	ЖΙ	6
4	Ж ΙΙΙ	8
5	ΙΙΙ	3

The lowest score is 2.

The highest score is 5.

The **mode**, or most frequent score, is 4.

Displaying data

It is useful to display data on a graph.

Colour	Tally	Frequency
Red	Ж Ж Ж ΙΙΙ	18
Blue	Ж Ж ΙΙΙ	13
Green	Ж Ж	10
White	Ж ΙΙΙ	8
Black	Ж Ι	6
Silver	ΙΙΙ	3

Colour of cars

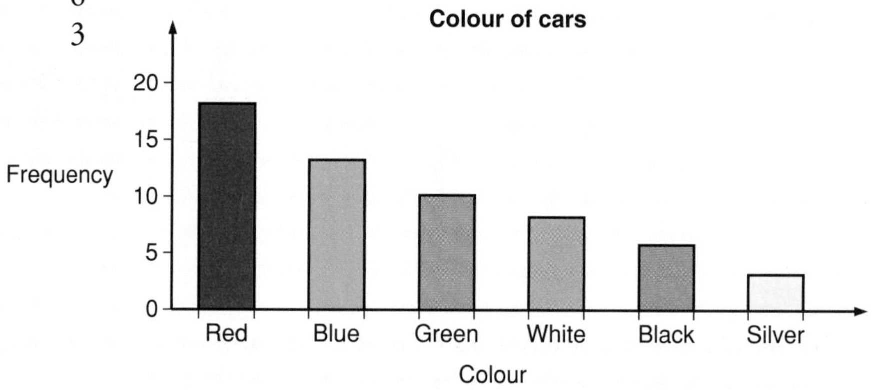

The mean

The **mean** is a type of average.

To find the mean: • calculate the total

• divide the total by the number of pieces of data.

5   6   8   0   1

5 pieces of data.

Total = 5 + 6 + 8 + 0 + 1 = 20

Mean = 20 ÷ 5 = **4**

15 3D shape

In this chapter you will review solid shapes, make 3D models and use nets.

15.1 Vertices, edges and faces

Remember

These are some common three-dimensional shapes:

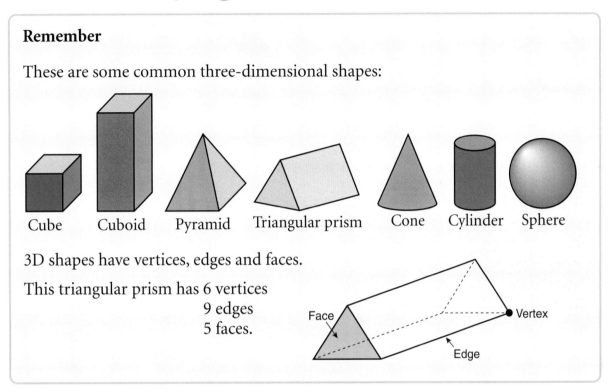

Cube Cuboid Pyramid Triangular prism Cone Cylinder Sphere

3D shapes have vertices, edges and faces.

This triangular prism has 6 vertices
9 edges
5 faces.

Exercise 15.1

1 Name the three-dimensional shapes you can see in each diagram.

2 In each diagram, use the word vertex, edge or face to name the green part.

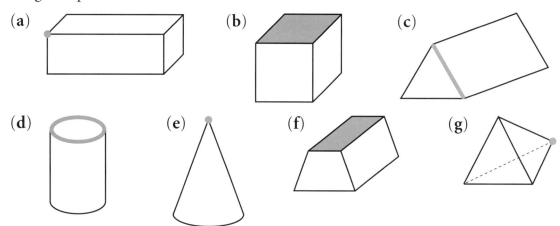

(a)   (b)   (c)

(d)   (e)   (f)   (g)

3 Copy and complete the table for each shape.

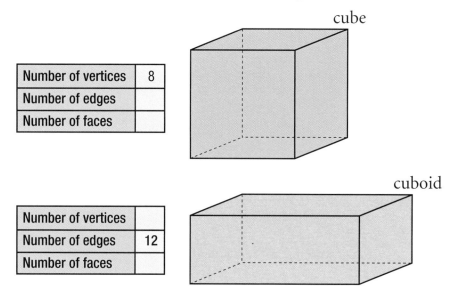

cube

Number of vertices	8
Number of edges	
Number of faces	

cuboid

Number of vertices	
Number of edges	12
Number of faces	

4 For each diagram, copy the table and complete the number of vertices, edges and faces.

(a)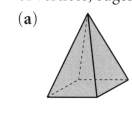

Number of vertices	
Number of edges	
Number of faces	

(b)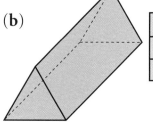

Number of vertices	
Number of edges	
Number of faces	

(c)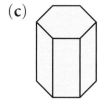

Number of vertices	
Number of edges	
Number of faces	

(d)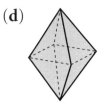

Number of vertices	
Number of edges	
Number of faces	

15.2 Skeleton models

Skeleton models of 3D shapes can be made using straws and pipe cleaners.

This cuboid has:

4 edges each 5 cm

4 edges each 6 cm

4 edges each 8 cm

8 vertices.

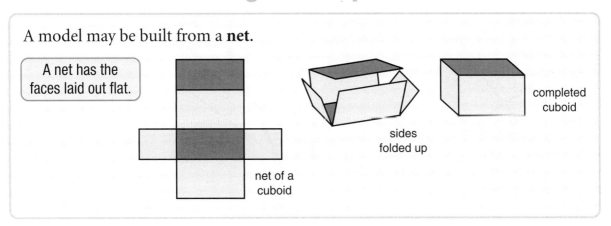

5 cm

6 cm

8 cm

Exercise 15.2

√ You need Worksheet **15.1** for questions **1** to **6**.

15.3 Nets – building 3D shapes

A model may be built from a **net**.

A net has the faces laid out flat.

net of a cuboid

sides folded up

completed cuboid

Exercise 15.3

√ You need Worksheets **15.2** and **15.3** for questions **1** to **4**.

15.4 Diagonals

A line joining two vertices on the same face of a 3D shape is a **diagonal**.

The diagonal on the red face is AC or CA.

A line joining two vertices not on the same face is called a **space diagonal**.

The green space diagonal is BH or HB.

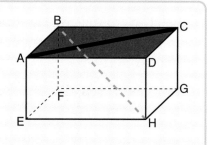

Exercise 15.4

W You need Worksheet **15.4** for questions **1** to **4**.

5 For each shape, name the diagonals shown.

(**a**)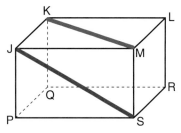

(**b**)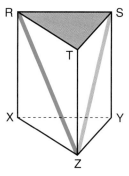

6 For each shape, name the space diagonals shown.

(**a**)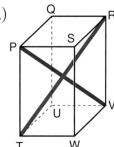

(**b**)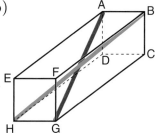

7 On the cube, the space diagonal PV has been drawn. Name the other three space diagonals.

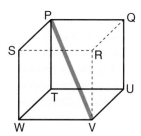

15.5 Angles

The angle shaded red is ∠PQW or ∠WQP.

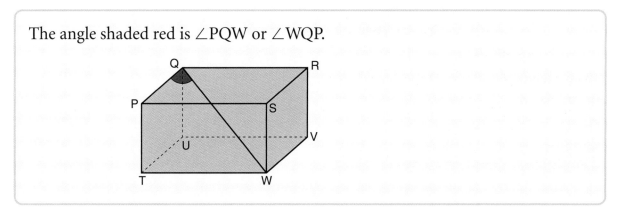

Exercise 15.5

1 On the cuboids shown, name:

(**a**) the blue angle

(**b**) the green angle.

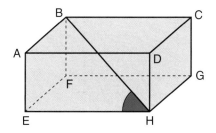

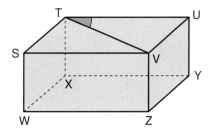

2 On the cuboid, name:

(**a**) the red angle

(**b**) the blue angle.

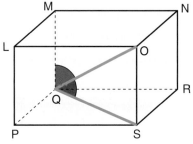

3 For each shape, name the blue angle.

(**a**)

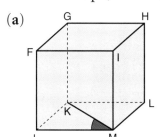

(**b**)

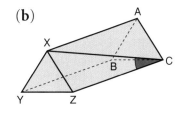

4 What colour is:

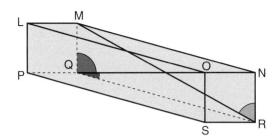

(**a**) ∠RQO

(**b**) ∠OQM

(**c**) ∠MRN?

Review exercise 15

1 In each diagram, use the word vertex, edge or face to name the green part.

(**a**) 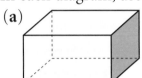   (**b**)    (**c**)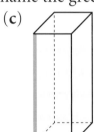

2 Copy and complete the table for each shape.

(**a**) 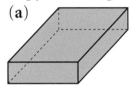   (**b**) 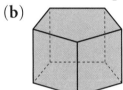   (**c**)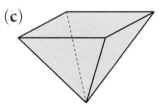

Number of vertices	
Number of edges	
Number of faces	

Number of vertices	
Number of edges	
Number of faces	

Number of vertices	
Number of edges	
Number of faces	

3 Pair each shape with its net.

A 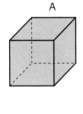   B   C 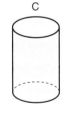   D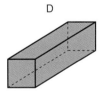

1 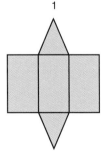   2 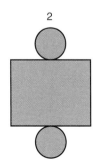   3 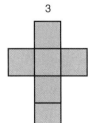   4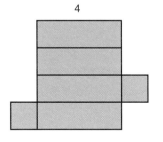

4 (**a**) Name the diagonals drawn on the
   top face of the cuboid.

(**b**) Which of the following could be
   drawn to make a diagonal:

   AD, HG, DG or AG?

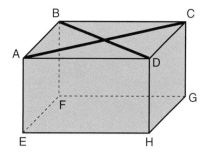

5 (**a**) Name the space diagonals drawn
   in this cuboid.

(**b**) Which of the following could be
   drawn to make another space
   diagonal:

   EA, FC, DG or EC?

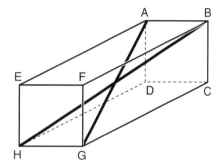

6 For each shape, name the blue angle.

(**a**)

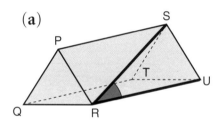

(**b**)

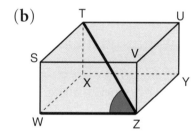

Vertices, edges and faces

This cuboid has: 8 vertices
12 edges
6 faces.

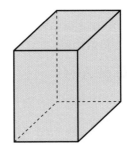

Nets

The net of a 3D shape has the sides laid out flat.

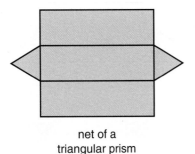

net of a
triangular prism

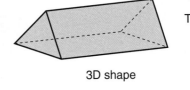

Triangular
prism

3D shape

Diagonals

A line joining two vertices on the same face is a **diagonal**.

A line joining two vertices not on the same face is a **space diagonal**.

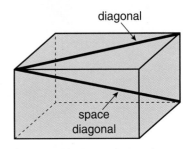

diagonal

space
diagonal

Angles

The angle shaded red is $\angle$PQW or $\angle$WQP.

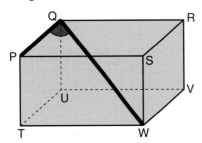

16 Problem solving

1 **Team selection**
Each team has 3 players.
One student has to be chosen from **each** age group.
List all the possible teams.

2 The map shows Strathben town centre.
Use the information to find each person's **starting point**.

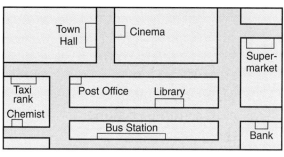

(**a**) Eilidh
Destination: Bank
Route:
• second right
• first left

(**b**) Calum
Destination: Supermarket
Route:
• first left
• second right

(**c**) Catriona
Destination: Cinema
Route:
• first left
• second right
• first left

3 Steven is solving Eli's number puzzles.

Find Eli's number for each of these puzzles.

(**a**) I think of a number, double it, then take away 3.
The result is 21.
What is my number?

(**b**) I think of a number, halve it, then add 3.
The result is 7.
What is my number?

You need A4 paper, a ruler and compasses.

4 (**a**) Follow these steps to draw a parabola.

Step 1

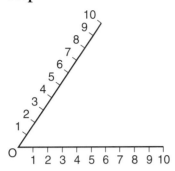

Step 2

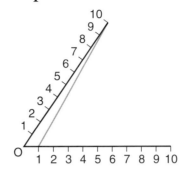

Step 3

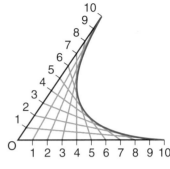

- Draw an angle with arms 10 cm long.
- Mark and number each centimetre along the arms.

- Join point 1 on one arm to point 10 on the other.

- Join points 2 to 9, 3 to 8 and so on.
- Draw the smooth curve shown by the red line.

> The curve you have drawn is called the **envelope** of the lines.
> This envelope is in the shape of a **parabola**.

(**b**) Follow these steps to draw another envelope.

Step 1

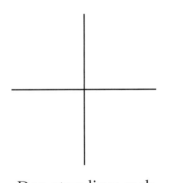

Step 2

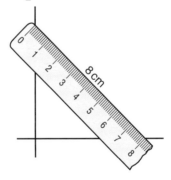

Step 3

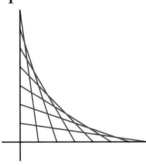

- Draw two lines each 16 cm long, which bisect each other at right angles.

- In the top right-hand quarter of the diagram, draw a line 8 cm long as shown.

- Draw more lines each 8 cm long.

Step 4

- Repeat Step 3 in each of the other quarters of your diagram.
- Draw the envelope of your lines.

This envelope is called an **astroid**.

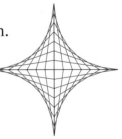

5 (**a**) • Copy the cross on 1 centimetre squared paper and cut it out.
  • Cut along the **red** lines.
  • Fit the 4 pieces together to form a square.
  • Draw the square to show how the pieces fit.

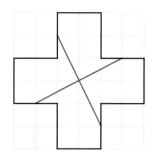

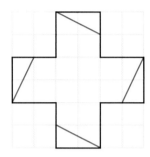

(**b**) • Copy the cross on 1 centimetre squared paper and cut it out.
  • Cut along the **red** lines.
  • Fit the 5 pieces together to form a square.
  • Draw the square to show how the pieces fit.

(**c**) • Copy this diagram on 1 centimetre squared paper and cut it out.
  • Cut along the **red** lines to make 4 congruent pieces.
  • Fit the pieces together to form **two** crosses.
  • Draw a cross to show how the pieces fit.

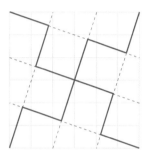

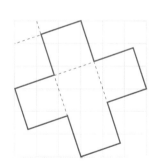

(**d**) • Copy this diagram on 1 centimetre squared paper and cut it out.
  • Cut along the **red** lines to make one cross and four pentagons.
  • Fit the pentagons together to form another cross.
  • Show how the pieces fit to make the second cross.

(**e**) • In the middle of a sheet of 1 centimetre squared paper draw a tile as shown.
  • Extend the pattern in all directions to make a tessellation of identical tiles.
  • Colour any **crosses** you find in the tessellation.

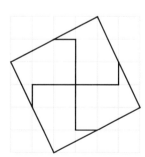

6 A cylinder, a triangular prism and a square
pyramid are on the table.

This is Meg's view or **elevation**.

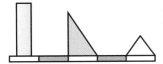

She sees the square pyramid on her right
and the cylinder on her left.

Who can see each of these elevations?

(**a**) 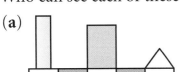   (**b**)    (**c**)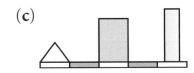

7 (**a**) The cylinder is moved to this position.

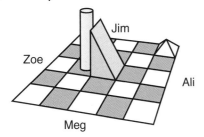

This is Ali's elevation.

Draw and label the elevations
seen by each of the others.

Draw and label each person's elevation for these positions.

(**b**) 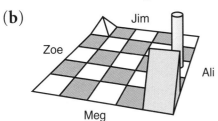   (**c**)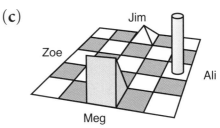

The shapes are moved again to give these elevations.

Meg's elevation

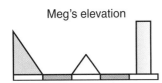

Ali's elevation

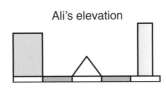

Draw the elevations for Zoe and Jim.

Answers

Chapter 1

Exercise 1.1

1 (a) 4650   (b) 12 600   (c) 8201   (d) 16 572
  (e) 596 000   (f) 221 405   (g) 603 007   (h) 2 432 000

2 Five hundred and forty-one thousand; three hundred and seven thousand, six hundred; one million, five hundred and twenty-eight thousand, four hundred and seven; five million, nine thousand, one hundred and twelve

3 (a) 7650   (b) 15 800   (c) 80 620
  (d) 4 300 000   (e) 5 780 200   (f) 603 000
  (g) 1 736 020   (h) 250 463   (i) 7 523 640

4 Highland: two hundred and eight thousand, nine hundred and fourteen
Edinburgh: four hundred and forty-eight thousand, six hundred and twenty-four
Dundee: one hundred and forty-five thousand, six hundred and sixty-three
Dumfries and Galloway: one hundred and forty-seven thousand, seven hundred and sixty five
Eilean Siar: twenty-six thousand, five hundred and two
Glasgow: five hundred and seventy-seven thousand, eight hundred and sixty-nine
Aberdeen: two hundred and twelve thousand, one hundred and twenty-five

5 B Goode: Six thousand, three hundred pounds
J Walker: £8427
T Please: £10 200
J Bell: One hundred and twenty-four thousand, six hundred and twelve pounds

6 (a) One hundred and thirty-nine thousand, five hundred and sixteen kilometres
(b) Forty-five thousand, four hundred and thirty-two kilometres
(c) Four thousand, eight hundred and sixty-six kilometres
(d) Two thousand, two hundred and seventy-four kilometres
(e) Six thousand, seven hundred and sixty kilometres
(f) Twelve thousand, one hundred and six kilometres

7 (a) 16 583   (b) 14 143   (c) 24 050   (d) 26 600
  (e) 74 000   (f) 62 000   (g) 8 800 000   (h) 7 500 000
  (i) 17 700   (j) 12 600

Exercise 1.2

1 (a) 204, 210, 217, 225, 232
(b) 400, 900, 1200, 1700, 1900, 2100
(c) 8096, 8107, 8113, 8117, 8122
(d) 21 150, 21 400, 21 550, 21 700, 21 950
(e) 15 898, 15 906, 15 914, 15 923, 15 929

2 (a) 1296   (b) 1304   (c) 1316
(d) 2300   (e) 3400   (f) 4100
(g) 10 300   (h) 10 550   (i) 10 850
(j) 13 930   (k) 13 965   (l) 13 990
(m)108 000   (n) 144 000   (o) 152 000

3 (a) 4652   (b) 4665   (c) 3879
(d) 3890   (e) 1105   (f) 1125
(g) 15 400   (h) 15 800   (i) 16 100
(j) 40 000   (k) 45 000   (l) 604 000
(m)607 000   (n) 610 000

4 (a) 106, 109, 117, 134, 143, 150
(b) 2006, 2067, 2100, 2600, 2650
(c) 15 000, 15 090, 15 100, 16 093, 16 500, 17 100
(d) 230 000, 240 000, 340 000, 360 000, 540 000
(e) 846 300, 846 372, 847 000, 847 900, 850 000
(f) 107 000, 107 300, 108 500, 110 000, 113 650, 127 000

5 6047, 6108, 6130, 6134, 6157, 6207, 6309, 6312, 6322, 6510

6 Pluto, Mercury, Mars, Venus, Earth, Neptune, Uranus, Saturn, Jupiter

7 3018, 3093, 3196, 3576, 3789, 3983, 4409

8 26 502, 48 077, 106 764, 120 235, 208 914, 226 871, 577 869

9 Scotland *v* France: Celtic Park
Spain *v* Portugal: Ibrox
England *v* Poland: Fir Park
Germany *v* Holland: McDiarmid Park
Italy *v* Denmark: Pittodrie or Tynecastle
Czech Republic *v* Estonia: Tynecastle or Pittodrie

Exercise 1.3

1 (a) 50   (b) 10   (c) 90   (d) 50
  (e) 100   (f) 240   (g) 390   (h) 210
  (i) 4890   (j) 6480

2 (a) 400   (b) 800   (c) 700   (d) 1000
  (e) 1200   (f) 1400   (g) 2600   (h) 3800

3 (a) 400   (b) 700   (c) 600   (d) 200   (e) 200
  (f) 400   (g) 700   (h) 500   (i) 700   (j) 1300
  (k) 4700   (l) 3200   (m) 6000   (n) 2600   (o) 2600
  (p) 4400   (q) 100   (r) 22 100   (s) 37 600   (t) 20 000

4 (a) 700   (b) 1300   (c) 1200
  (d) 1000   (e) 600   (f) 600
  (g) 700   (h) 800   (i) 1300

5 Willing: 1500; Wirt: 1200; Barker: 2600; Binghamton: 4800; Colesville: 5300; Conklin: 5900; Dickinson: 5100; Fenton: 6800; Kirkwood: 5800; Lisle: 2300; Maine: 5300; Nanticoke: 1700; Sanford: 2400; Triangle: 2900; Windsor: 6100; Allegany: 8500; Ward: 300; West Almond: 300

6 (a) 3020, 3980, 4410, 3790, 3090, 3200, 3580, 3290, 3220, 3060
(b) 3000, 4000, 4400, 3800, 3100, 3200, 3600, 3300, 3200, 3100

7 (a) 1000   (b) 2000   (c) 3000   (d) 6000
  (e) 9000   (f) 7000   (g) 5000   (h) 5000

Exercise 1.4

1 (a) (estimate 50 + 30 = 80); 78
(b) (estimate 60 + 120 = 180); 181
(c) (estimate 150 + 210 = 360); 361
(d) (estimate 240 + 190 = 430); 425

2 (a) (estimate 60 − 50 = 10); 15
(b) (estimate 250 − 70 = 180); 176
(c) (estimate 470 − 260 = 210); 215
(d) (estimate 810 − 340 = 470); 476

3 (a) 93   (b) 34   (c) 813
  (d) 53   (e) 103   (f) 383

4 (a) 353   (b) 610   (c) 460
  (d) 1180   (e) 2744   (f) 3812

5 £455

6 £485

7 1511 cubic metres

8 4410 km

9 £415

10 22 050 km

11 £1009

12 (a) £354   (b) £411   (c) £490

13 (a) 4150 cm   (b) 850 cm

14 £125

Exercise 1.5

1 (a) 135   (b) 72   (c) 504
  (d) 294   (e) 201   (f) 252

2 (a) 645   (b) 785   (c) 1820
  (d) 828   (e) 1920   (f) 2736

3 £620

4 576

5 2450 g flour, 595 g ground almonds, 1225 g sugar, 21 eggs, 875 ml milk

6 (a) £192   (b) £495   (c) £1494   (d) £352
   (e) 4 nights at Glenbeagles
7 (a) £183   (b) £471   (c) £1280
8 £1143
9 £5888

Exercise 1.6

1 (a) 150   (b) 360   (c) 1530
   (d) 2040   (e) 17 060   (f) 5000
2 (a) 3600   (b) 80 700   (c) 19 600
   (d) 600 000   (e) 103 000   (f) 4700
3 (a) 2860   (b) 3400   (c) 20 700
   (d) 31 000   (e) 19 990   (f) 50 300
4 (a) 150 g   (b) 1560 g   (c) 35 000 g
5 (a) 30 mm   (b) 120 mm   (c) 870 mm   (d) 2830 mm
6 (a) 4000 cm   (b) 13 600 cm   (c) 50 000 cm   (d) 73 600 cm
7 £1650
8 £2940
9 (a) £5400   (b) £12 800   (c) £30 600   (d) £3600
10 (a) 450   (b) 5000   (c) 6800   (d) 10 000

Exercise 1.7

1 (a) 14   (b) 38   (c) 16
   (d) 21   (e) 44   (f) 32
2 (a) 24   (b) 34   (c) 49
   (d) 75   (e) 83   (f) 337
3 £1625
4 39 metres
5 £600
6 325
7 29
8 70 g flour, 15 g butter, 25 g sugar
9 Corfu: £97
   Kos: £94
   Prague: £86

Exercise 1.8

1 (a) 47   (b) 36   (c) 52
   (d) 800   (e) 240   (f) 3800
2 (a) 16   (b) 23   (c) 33
   (d) 42   (e) 640   (f) 500
3 (a) 27   (b) 52   (c) 720
   (d) 60   (e) 2740   (f) 350
4 2 kg
5 25
6 12
7 £102

Exercise 1.9

1 (a) 17   (b) 7   (c) 34   (d) 20
   (e) 17   (f) 13   (g) 8   (h) 19
   (i) 8   (j) 18   (k) 3   (l) 23
2 (a) $4 \times 3 + 2 = 14$
   (b) $10 + 3 \times 2 = 16$
   (c) $20 \div 2 + 3 = 13$
   (d) $4 \times 5 - 7 = 13$
   (e) $2 + 4 \times 3 = 14$
   (f) $5 \times 5 + 1 = 26$

Exercise 1.10

1 8
2 6
3 5
4 (a) 5   (b) 4
5 (a) 16   (b) 3 cm
6 (a) 8   (b) 1

Exercise 1.11

1 (a) 61   (b) 42   (c) 41
   (d) 34   (e) 61   (f) 101
   (g) 118   (h) 91   (i) 122
2 (a) 12   (b) 25   (c) 9
   (d) 26   (e) 9   (f) 15
   (g) 18   (h) 45   (i) 19
3 91p
4 27p
5 17
6 56 cm

Review Exercise 1

1 (a) 6250   (b) 24 700   (c) 41 634   (d) 4 836 000
2 (a) 104, 108, 114, 120, 136, 154
   (b) 3004, 3012, 3020, 3036, 3057
   (c) 12 005, 12 400, 13 090, 13 093, 14 100, 14 600
   (d) 216 000, 216 012, 216 040, 216 153, 216 200
3 (a) 500   (b) 200   (c) 500   (d) 300
   (e) 100   (f) 700   (g) 1300   (h) 2300
4 (a) 272   (b) 336   (c) 47   (d) 422
   (e) 736   (f) 1170   (g) 551   (h) 34
5 (a) £83
   (b) £98, free postage
   (c) £78
6 84
7 £7275
8 (a) 270   (b) 5000   (c) 30 500
   (d) 31 400   (e) 2600   (f) 35 060
9 (a) 26   (b) 46   (c) 380
   (d) 70   (e) 7140   (f) 950
10 10
11 (a) 41
   (b) 2 cm
12 (a) 112
   (b) 896

Chapter 2

Exercise 2.1

1 B(1, 4); C(0, 2); D(5, 0); E(2, 5); F(4, 5); G(5, 3); H(3, 3); J(0, 1);
   K(3, 0); L(7, 5); M(6, 2); N(5, 0); P(1, 2); Q(0, 5); R(10, 0)
2 (a) City: (0, 7); Town: (6, 4); Harbour: (3, 10); Rock: (1, 5);
     Scary Tower: (6, 6); Lighthouse: (11, 1); Cave: (11, 10);
     Village: (3, 0); Hill: (4, 7); Swamp: (9, 8)
   (b) (5, 1) on map
3 A(2, 1); B(3, 5); C(5, 1); D(1, 2); E(5, 0); F(4, 4); G(3, 0); H(4, 5);
   J(0, 4); K(3, 1); L(1, 1); M(3, 3); N(1, 5); P(1, 0); Q(0, 1); R(6, 0);
   S(1, 5); T(0, 0); U(3, 2); V(6, 4); W(8, 3); Z(10, 1)

Exercise 2.2

1

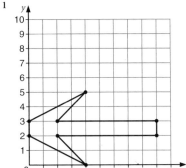

2

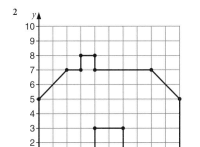

3

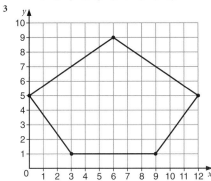

4

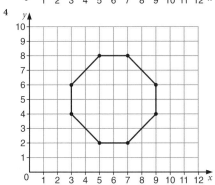

5 (a) Rectangle
(b) 5 units (c) 2 units (d) 5 units (e) 2 units

6 (a) Triangle, square
(b) 4 units (c) 4 units (d) 2 units (e) 3 units
(f) 3 units (g) 3 units (h) 3 units

7 (a-b)

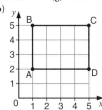

(c) Rectangle
(d) 3 units

8 (a-b)

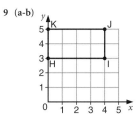

(c) Triangle
(d) 4 units
(e) 5 units

9 (a-b)

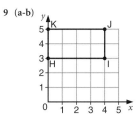

(c) K(0, 5)
(d) (i) 2 units (ii) 4 units

10 (a) 7
(b)

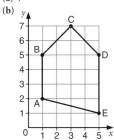

(c) Pentagon

11 (a)   ; rocket

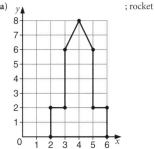

(b)   ; triangular prism

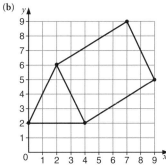

(c)   ; arrow

(d)   ; ship

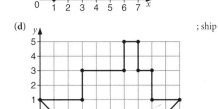

12

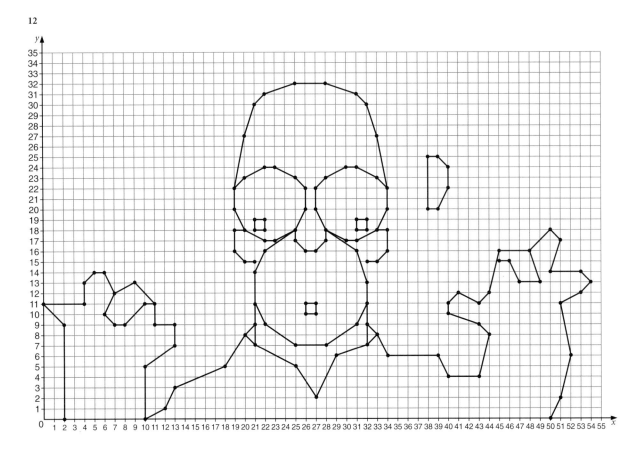

Exercise 2.3

1 **(a)** Go forward 2 squares. Turn left.
Forward 2 squares. Turn right.
Forward 3 squares. Turn right.
Forward 2 squares. Turn left, then forward 2 squares.
(b) Forward 3 squares. Turn left.
Forward 2 squares. Turn right.
Forward 2 squares. Turn right.
Forward 1 square. Turn left, then forward 2 squares.
(c) Forward 2 squares. Turn right.
Forward 2 squares. Turn right.
Forward 1 square. Turn left.
Forward 1 square. Turn left.
Forward 3 squares. Turn left.
Forward 2 squares. Turn right.
Forward 1 square. Turn right.
Forward 1 square. Turn left, then forward 2 squares.

2

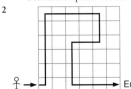

3 **(a)** Forward 3 squares. Turn left.
Forward 2 squares. Turn right.
Forward 2 squares. Turn right.
Forward 1 square. Turn left.
Forward 1 square, then end.
(b) Forward 2 squares. Turn right.
Forward 2 squares. Turn right.
Forward 1 square. Turn left.

Forward 1 square. Turn left.
Forward 3 squares. Turn left.
Forward 2 squares. Turn right.
Forward 1 square. Turn right.
Forward 1 square. Turn left.
Forward 1 square, then end.

4

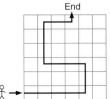

5 Bank to the shop: I come out of the bank. Turn right. Walk forward
and turn second right. Take second left. Enter the shop on the right.
Post office to the shop: I come out of the post office. Turn left. Walk
forward and turn first left. Take second left. Enter the shop on the
right.
Baker to shop: I come out of the bakers. Turn left. Walk forward and
turn first left. Cross the road and enter the shop on the left.
Baker to the bank: I come out of the bakers. Turn right. Walk
forward and turn first right. Take third right. Take third left. Enter
the bank on the left.

Review exercise 2

1 A(0, 0), B(2, 4), C(3, 0), D(7, 5), E(5, 4), F(9, 0), G(10, 5)
2 **(a)** (1, 12)   **(b)** (4, 10)   **(c)** (9, 10)
   (d) (0, 9)   **(e)** (6, 7)   **(f)** (12, 5)
   (g) (8, 4)   **(h)** (6, 3)   **(i)** (5, 5)
   (j) (0, 5)   **(k)** (2, 0)   **(l)** (10, 0)
   (m) (0, 2)   **(n)** (7, 0)

3

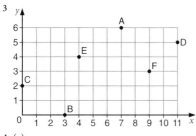

4 (a)

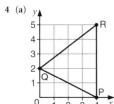

(b) Triangle

5 (a)

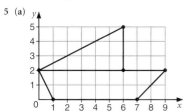

(b) Yacht

6 (a)

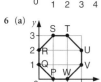

(b) Octagon

7 (a) (b)

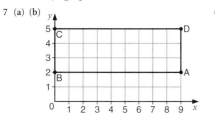

(c) D(9, 5)

8 Forward 3 squares. Turn right.
Forward 2 squares. Turn left.
Forward 2 squares. Turn left.
Forward 1 square. Turn right.
Forward 1 square, then end.

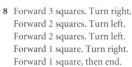

Chapter 3

Exercise 3.1

1 (a) 0·1 **(b)** $\frac{5}{10}$ **(c)** 0·6 **(d)** $\frac{2}{10}$
(e) Whole diagram shaded
(f) $\frac{7}{10}$, 0·7 **(g)** $\frac{4}{10}$, 0·4 **(h)** $\frac{3}{10}$, 0·3 **(i)** $\frac{8}{10}$, 0·8

2 (a)

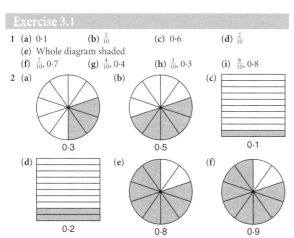

(g)

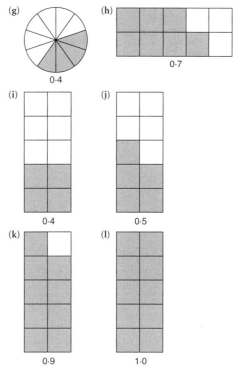

(i)

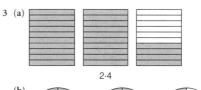

(k)

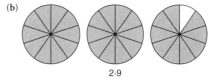

3 (a)

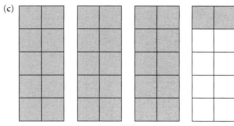

(c)

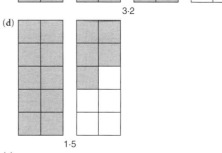

(e)

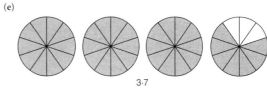

(f)

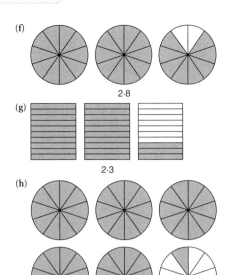

2·8

(g)

2·3

(h)

5·1

4 (a) 3·2   (b) 4·5   (c) 4·7   (d) 1·1
   (e) 0·9   (f) 3·4   (g) 2·8   (h) 1·3
5 (a) 0·3   (b) 0·4   (c) 0
   (d) 0·3   (e) 0·5   (f) 0·2
6 (a) 0·7   (b) 0·3   (c) 0·8
   (d) 0·6   (e) 0·6   (f) 0·9
   (g) 0·7   (h) 0·8   (i) 0·2

Exercise 3.2

1 (a) 0·03   (b) $\frac{4}{100}$ (c) 0·30
   (d) $\frac{20}{100}$ (e) 0·57   (f) $\frac{45}{100}$
   (g) $\frac{68}{100}$, 0·68   (h) 0·12   (i) $\frac{28}{100}$, 0·28
2 (a)

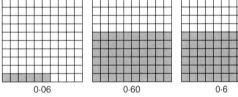

0·06   0·60   0·6

  (b)

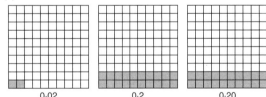

0·02   0·2   0·20

  (c)

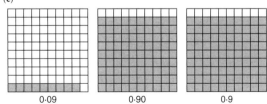

0·09   0·90   0·9

3 (a) 0·27   (b) 0·08   (c) 0·03
   (d) 0·51   (e) 0·72   (f) 0·43
   (g) 0·4   (h) 0·24   (i) 0·88
   (j) 1·3   (k) 2·75   (l) 2·08
   (m) 1·03

Exercise 3.3

1 (a) 8 tenths   (b) 8 hundredths   (c) 8 hundredths
   (d) 8 units   (e) 8 tenths   (f) 8 tenths
   (g) 8 tens   (h) 8 tenths
2 (a) 1   (b) 2   (c) 2   (d) 1
   (e) 2   (f) 2   (g) 1   (h) 2
3 (a) 2·8, 3·7, 4·4, 5·0, 5·6
   (b) 7·6, 8·5, 9·2, 10·1, 10·8
   (c) 0·1, 0·7, 2·9, 3·5, 4·0
4 (a) 2·8, 3·0, 3·6, 4·4, 5·1
   (b) 8·9, 9·4, 10·9, 11·5, 12·0, 12·9
   (c) 19·7, 20·5, 21·6, 22·3, 23·0, 23·8
   (d) 0·8, 1·7, 2·3, 3·1, 3·5, 4·2, 4·6
5 (a) 0·08, 0·16, 0·25, 0·30, 0·37
   (b) 0·96, 1·05, 1·12, 1·21, 1·28
   (c) 2·05, 2·12, 2·20, 2·28, 2·37
6 (a) 2·54, 2·65, 2·76, 2·91, 2·99
   (b) 0·88, 0·96, 1·04, 1·14, 1·23, 1·29
   (c) 3·98, 4·08, 4·13, 4·25, 4·36, 4·41
   (d) 0·01, 0·06, 0·18, 0·24, 0·31, 0·37
7 (a) 1·4   (b) 2·2   (c) 2·9
   (d) 3·7   (e) 4·4   (f) 6·9
   (g) 7·5   (h) 8·2   (i) 9
   (j) 9·4   (k) 9·9   (l) 6·41
   (m) 6·5   (n) 6·57   (o) 6·65
   (p) 6·69   (q) 6·74

Exercise 3.4

1 (a) 3·5   (b) 2·8   (c) 2·8
   (d) 3·5   (e) 2·5   (f) 3·5
   (g) 2·8   (h) 2·6   (i) 3·2
2 (a) 5·6   (b) 2·9   (c) 3·1
   (d) 8·0   (e) 3·5   (f) 6·6
3 (a) 4·1, 4·3, 4·7, 5·0, 5·7, 5·8, 6·2, 6·4
   (b) 0·2, 0·8, 0·9, 1·2, 1·5, 3·0, 3·4, 3·5
   (c) 16·1, 16·3, 16·9, 17·1, 17·5, 17·9, 18·0, 18·2
   (d) 53·2, 53·5, 53·9, 54, 54·2, 54·7, 55·1, 55·6
   (e) 29·2, 29·4, 29·8, 30·0, 30·7, 31·1, 31·9, 32·3
4 (a) 7·5, 7·8, 8·0, 8·2, 8·6, 8·9, 9·1, 9·3
   (b) 16·7, 16·9, 17·0, 17·4, 17·5, 17·8, 17·9
   (c) 3·0, 3·2, 3·5, 3·7, 4·2, 4·5, 4·7
   (d) 1·7, 1·9, 2·0, 2·3, 2·7, 2·9, 3·1, 3·3
   (e) 0·3, 0·4, 0·6, 0·7, 0·9, 1·0, 1·1, 1·2, 1·5

Exercise 3.5

1 (a) £1.52   (b) £3.47   (c) £2.60
   (d) £5.10   (e) £7.20   (f) £6.30
2 (a) 1·52   (b) 3·47   (c) 2·60
   (d) 5·10   (e) 7·20   (f) 6·30
3 (a) 4·7   (b) 4·83   (c) 5·21   (d) 4·2
   (e) 4·34   (f) 4·6   (g) 4·5   (h) 5·1
   (i) 4·85   (j) 4·45   (k) 4·1   (l) 4·1
4 (a) 11·5   (b) 16·35   (c) 18·71
   (d) 15·5   (e) 30·31   (f) 27·8
5 (a) £1.08, £1.09, £1.10, £1.31, £1.54, £1.64, £1.90
   (b) £3.06, £3.14, £3.15, £3.20, £3.54, £3.72
   (c) £11.48, £11.60, £11.70, £12.02, £12.14, £12.32, £12.50
   (d) £20.07, £20.09, £20.10, £20.14, £20.18, £20.25, £20.40
6 (a) 0·02, 0·07, 0·2, 0·21, 0·25, 0·31, 0·39
   (b) 0·4, 0·45, 0·52, 0·56, 0·58, 0·6, 0·61, 0·67
   (c) 0·05, 0·1, 0·14, 0·16, 0·24, 0·35, 0·39, 0·5
   (d) 1·07, 1·21, 1·50, 1·57, 1·6, 1·63, 1·71, 1·77
   (e) 4·98, 5·07, 5·18, 5·43, 5·65, 5·70, 5·75, 5·84
7 (a) 3·5, 3·59, 3·6, 3·61, 3·67, 3·74
   (b) 4·07, 4·27, 4·36, 4·6, 5·1, 5·7, 5·84
   (c) 7·11, 7·14, 7·36, 7·45, 7·69, 7·8
   (d) 5·03, 5·1, 5·18, 5·3, 5·31, 5·46
   (e) 9·14, 9·4, 9·78, 10·06, 10·1, 10·32, 10·77

Exercise 3.6

1 (a) 5   (b) 3   (c) 9   (d) 8
   (e) 13   (f) 21   (g) 20   (h) 57
   (i) 140   (j) 159
2 (a) 7   (b) 4   (c) 2   (d) 8
   (e) 13   (f) 11   (g) 27   (h) 11
   (i) 1   (j) 14   (k) 9   (l) 23
3 Silicon: 19; Iron: 14; Titanium: 6; Aluminium: 6; Magnesium: 5

Exercise 3.7

1 (a) 4 + 18 = 22 cm
   (b) 10 + 3 + 5 = 18 cm
   (c) 3 + 10 = 13 cm
   (d) 6 + 1 + 4 = 11 cm
2 7 + 12 = 19 kg
3 6 − 3 = 3 m

Exercise 3.8

1 (a) 0·2   (b) 5·4   (c) 7·9   (d) 3·7
   (e) 0·8   (f) 17·5   (g) 30·0   (h) 12·6
   (i) 1·0   (j) 32·2
2 (a) 6·4   (b) 3·8   (c) 5·8   (d) 1·4
   (e) 5·8   (f) 8·2   (g) 12·3   (h) 21·5
   (i) 16·9   (j) 4·3   (k) 11·0   (l) 18·1
   (m) 9·9   (n) 10·0   (o) 10·1   (p) 15·4
3 39·2, 39·2, 39·2, 40·0, 40·3, 39·6, 40·1, 39·9, 41·0
4 0·8, 0·3, 0·8, 2·0, 1·0, 0·7
5 0·4, 0·7, 0·5, 0·3, 0·7, 59·8, 6·1, 0·5, 1·1
6 Male: 45·0, 45·4, 42·6, 42·7, 41·6, 41·6, 41·8, 42·6, 43·6, 44·6
   Female: 31·6, 32·3, 31·6, 31·8, 33·6, 33·5, 31·9, 31·7, 31·2, 30·3

Exercise 3.9

1 (a) 0·5   (b) 0·8   (c) 0·1
   (d) 0·2   (e) 0·3   (f) 0·1
   (g) 0·8   (h) 0·5   (i) 1·0
2 (a) 2·9   (b) 3·8   (c) 8·5
   (d) 9·9   (e) 6·9   (f) 2·9
   (g) 8·8   (h) 2·9   (i) 3·0
3 (a) 0·2   (b) 0·2   (c) 0·4
   (d) 0·4   (e) 0·3   (f) 1·1
   (g) 0·1   (h) 0·5   (i) 0·6
4 (a) 1·5   (b) 1·6   (c) 1·2
   (d) 2·5   (e) 1·0   (f) 0·8
   (g) 1·4   (h) 2·1   (i) 0
5 (a) 3·1   (b) 1·7   (c) 0·8   (d) 2·2
   (e) 1·2   (f) 6·2   (g) 1·9   (h) 3·1
   (i) 0·5   (j) 1·2   (k) 2·7   (l) 2·0
6 0·7 kg
7 1·2 m
8 5·2 kg
9 0·8°C

Exercise 3.10

1 (a) 10·1   (b) 8·6   (c) 10·53   (d) 19·0
   (e) 86·1   (f) 36·1   (g) 78·5   (h) 73·3
   (i) 52·79   (j) 40·52   (k) 66·14   (l) 68·40
2 (a) 1·8   (b) 0·5   (c) 8·9   (d) 21·8
   (e) 25·59   (f) 14·78   (g) 13·4   (h) 35·3
   (i) 13·49   (j) 9·32   (k) 12·06   (l) 16·73
3 10·8 kg
4 £6.02
5 £6.49
6 £26.14
7 1·46 m
8 7·2°C
9 85·1 cm
10 Pupils' own answers

Exercise 3.11 (continued)

11 (a) 273·3 kg
   (b) 26·7 kg
   (c) No, because she will take the total weight over 300kg
12 (a) £3.65 + £6.95 + £4.10 = £14.70
   (b) Mr Benson: £15.65; Mrs Benson: £16.30; Angela: £15.35;
     Total: £47.30

Exercise 3.11

1 (a) 9   (b) 10·8   (c) 41·5   (d) 71·2
   (e) 274·2   (f) 453·6   (g) 130·0   (h) 382·2
   (i) 196·0   (j) 431·9   (k) 172·80   (l) 74·04
   (m) 12·75   (n) 7·14   (o) 56·64   (p) 183·6
   (q) 140·56   (r) 123·04   (s) 60·24   (t) 103·92
2 £27.20
3 12 metres
4 (a) 10·5 litres   (b) £7.63
5 (a) £15.90   (b) 90p
6 £80.55
7 (a) £8.97   (b) £7.00   (c) £15.97
8 (a) £3.62   (b) 28p   (c) £6.60

Exercise 3.12

1 (a) 18·7   (b) 16·3   (c) 24·6   (d) 2·3
   (e) 14·6   (f) 14·5   (g) 22·4   (h) 67·5
   (i) 13·6   (j) 27·5   (k) 23·4   (l) 12·3
2 (a) 12·53   (b) 52·3   (c) 12·58
   (d) 8·54   (e) 0·46   (f) 8·15
   (g) 14·52   (h) 3·75   (i) 3·25
3 4·7 kg
4 40p
5 19·1 kg
6 1·4 kg
7 £20.25
8 3·25 m

Exercise 3.13

1 (a) 41   (b) 32   (c) 68
   (d) 372   (e) 86   (f) 4
2 (a) 19·1   (b) 54·6   (c) 80·7
   (d) 5·3   (e) 6·7   (f) 513·8
3 (a) 27   (b) 31·2   (c) 5·6
   (d) 17·8   (e) 156·4   (f) 190·8
   (g) 120·3   (h) 13   (i) 7
4 (a) 820   (b) 170   (c) 420
   (d) 370   (e) 260   (f) 590
   (g) 2050   (h) 30   (i) 60
5 (a) 1717   (b) 1364   (c) 3805
   (d) 2275   (e) 647   (f) 801
   (g) 1020   (h) 45   (i) 22
6 (a) 452   (b) 236   (c) 5060
   (d) 258   (e) 630   (f) 57
   (g) 6250   (h) 365   (i) 92
   (j) 141   (k) 709   (l) 830·5
7 (a) 7 g   (b) 70 g
8 (a) £14.00
   (b) The Cash and Carry, because the cost per pen is less.
   (a) £873.80   (b) £1062.00

Exercise 3.14

1 (a) 4·7   (b) 6·3   (c) 8·8
   (d) 39   (e) 16·4   (f) 87
2 (a) 0·72   (b) 0·94   (c) 0·13
   (d) 0·05   (e) 4·06   (f) 3·68
3 (a) 0·07   (b) 0·14   (c) 1·59
   (d) 2·79   (e) 6·67   (f) 9·01
4 (a) 1·16   (b) 2·38   (c) 5·79   (d) 0·85
   (e) 0·15   (f) 0·60   (g) 0·78   (h) 3·56
   (i) 0·50   (j) 0·03   (k) 0·04   (l) 0·06

5 (a) 6·5   (b) 405·6   (c) 81
  (d) 2   (e) 2·86   (f) 4·3
  (g) 40·5   (h) 1·65   (i) 1·84
6 5·2 g
7 6·32 g
8 (a) £87.00   (b) £103.70   (c) £124.00
9 (a) 65   (b) 41·34   (c) 5174   (d) 2·5
  (e) 286   (f) 0·046   (g) 0·05   (h) 0·37
  (i) 560   (j) 0·08   (k) 0·8   (l) 0·09

Exercise 3.15

1 (a) £125.30   (b) £1352.40   (c) £6695.50   (d) £53.04
  (e) £1681.30   (f) £1439.30   (g) £4180.30   (h) £6807.45
2 (a) £5.44   (b) £10.50   (c) £14.40
  (d) £5.20   (e) £16.80
3 (a) £2246.68   (b) £3025.31   (c) £3074.19   (d) £4251.22
4 (a) £2.10 + £3.60 + £25.60 + £4.00 = £35.30
  (b) £13.92 + £3.45 + £1.82 + £4.90 = £24.09
5 £2 083 227.53
6 (a) 7·585   (b) 269·6   (c) 1606·28
  (d) 15·13   (e) 295·2   (f) 2569
  (g) 322·92   (h) 593·71   (i) 926·5
7 £7572.00
8 £33.60
9 (a) 80p   (b) £1.60   (c) £9.60
10 (a) 62·4   (b) 0·68   (c) 237 060
  (d) 0·502   (e) 1570   (f) 0·026
  (g) 0·13   (h) 1110   (i) 0·04

Exercise 3.16

1 14
2 14
3 6
4 (a) 28   (b) 1
5 (a) 8   (b) £2.00
6 32
7 8
8 11
9 (a) 6   (b) 2

Review Exercise 3

1 (a) 0·6   (b) 3·2
2 (a) 0·47   (b) 2·44
3 (a) 0·3   (b) 0·8   (c) 1·3   (d) 3·99
  (e) 4·02   (f) 4·07   (g) 4·11   (h) 4·19
4 (a) 3·8, 4·0, 4·8, 4·9, 5·1, 5·4, 5·5, 6·1
  (b) 10·0, 10·4, 11·1, 11·2, 11·7, 11·9, 12·8
  (c) 2·1, 2·14, 2·36, 2·69, 3·45, 3·8
  (d) 15·04, 15·1, 15·2, 15·31, 15·47, 15·48
5 (a) 3   (b) 3   (c) 11   (d) 12
6 (a) 5·4   (b) 1·8   (c) 14·0   (d) 25·5
7 (a) 2·5   (b) 1·9   (c) 6·0   (d) 3·6
8 (a) 13·08   (b) 15·4   (c) 102·54   (d) 34·5
9 (a) 218   (b) 2417   (c) 2116   (d) 1290
  (e) 102·7   (f) 3504   (g) 3·2   (h) 317·7
  (i) 0·76   (j) 0·7   (k) 1·35   (l) 73
10 (a) 8   (b) £3
11 7
12 £11.56
13 £45.15
14 £23.75
15 £6.76 + £6.00 + £5.76 + £16.80 + £6.00 = £41.32

Chapter 4

Exercise 4.1

2-3 Pupils' own answers

Exercise 4.2

1 Arms: ST and TV, Vertex: T, Name: STV
  Arms: XY and YZ, Vertex: Y, Name: XYZ
  Arms: GK and KL, Vertex: K, Name: GKL
  Arms: CM and HM, Vertex: M, Name: HMC
  Arms: HF and FG, Vertex: F, Name: HFG
  Arms: RT and TS, Vertex: T, Name: RTS
  Arms: QR and RT, Vertex: R, Name: QRT
  Arms: CA and BA, Vertex: A, Name: BAC
2 (a) ∠ABC   (b) ∠PTC   (c) ∠XYZ
  (d) ∠TUV   (e) ∠FDE
3 (a) ∠HFG   (b) ∠MLN   (c) ∠RTS   (d) ∠QRY
4 (a) ∠ABC   (b) ∠BAC   (c) ∠BCA
5 (a)   (b)

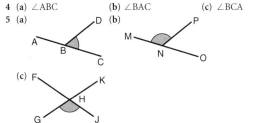

  (c)

6 (a) ∠ABC, ∠CDE
  (b) Examples are: ∠BHD, ∠BCD, ∠HDC, ∠GAB, ∠HBC, ∠DEF, ∠AGF
  (c) ∠XYZ, ∠SYZ, ∠STZ, ∠YZT, ∠YST, ∠TSV

Exercise 4.3

1 (a) (b)

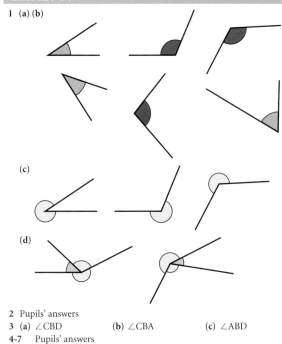

  (c)

  (d)

2 Pupils' answers
3 (a) ∠CBD   (b) ∠CBA   (c) ∠ABD
4-7 Pupils' answers

Exercise 4.4

1 (a) 30°   (b) 70°   (c) 100°   (d) 150°
2 (a) acute, 65°   (b) acute, 20°   (c) obtuse, 130°
  (d) obtuse, 95°   (e) acute, 45°   (f) obtuse, 115°
  (g) obtuse, 147°   (h) acute, 53°
3 (a) 145°   (b) 50°   (c) 15°
  (d) 125°   (e) 70°   (f) 42°
  (g) 85°   (h) 35°   (i) 168°
4 (a) acute, 44°   (b) acute, 21°   (c) acute, 58°
  (d) obtuse, 136°   (e) obtuse, 130°   (f) acute, 45°
  (g) acute, 70°   (h) acute, 140°   (i) obtuse, 112°

Exercise 4.5

1-3 Pupils' drawings

Exercise 4.6

1 (a) 60°   (b) 50°   (c) 55°
2 (a) 30°   (b) 40°   (c) 65°
   (d) 66°   (e) 12°   (f) 48°

Exercise 4.7

1 (a) 120°   (b) 50°   (c) 35°
2 (a) 120°   (b) 60°   (c) 115°
   (d) 55°   (e) 125°   (f) 65°
3 (a) obtuse, 143°   (b) acute, 36°   (c) obtuse, 113°
   (d) acute, 66°   (e) obtuse, 102°; acute, 67°

Exercise 4.8

1 Walk west until you reach the shop.
Turn north and walk past the shop.
Turn west and walk to the traffic lights.
Turn south and walk until you reach the bus station.
2 (a) School, church
   (b) Youth hostel
   (c) Castle, Visitor centre
   (d) Riding stables

Exercise 4.9

1 (a) Thurso   (b) Oban   (c) Dunfermline
   (d) Portree   (e) Glasgow   (f) Aberdeen
   (g) Dunbar
2 (a) north   (b) south west   (c) north west
   (d) south   (e) east   (f) south east
3 Portree
4 (a) 90°   (b) 45°   (c) 90°
   (d) 180°   (e) 135°   (f) 135°
5 (a) east   (b) south   (c) north east   (d) west

Exercise 4.10

1 (a) 000°   (b) 180°   (c) 090°
   (d) 270°   (e) 045°
2 (a) 050°   (b) 085°   (c) 115°
   (d) 160°   (e) 250°   (f) 320°
3 (a) 010°   (b) 045°   (c) 175°   (d) 315°
4 (a) 000°   (b) 040°   (c) 178°
   (d) 272°   (e) 305°   (f) 210°

Review Exercise 4

1 (a) ∕ STU, ∕ TUR, ∠URS, ∠RST
   (b) ∠EFG, ∠DFH, ∠EFH, ∠DFG
2

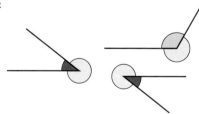

3 (a) 55°   (b) 107°
4 Pupils' drawings
5 (a) obtuse, 150°   (b) acute, 50°   (c) acute, 53°
6 (a) 2   (b) 1   (c) 3   (d) 5
7 (a) south   (b) north east   (c) east
8 (a) 090°   (b) 045°   (c) 180°   (d) 225°
9 (a) 055°   (b) 125°   (c) 235°

Chapter 5

Exercise 5.1

1 (a) $\frac{1}{4}$ (b) $\frac{3}{7}$ (c) $\frac{5}{9}$
   (d) 3\8   (e) $\frac{5}{12}$ (f) $\frac{7}{10}$
   (g) $\frac{5}{7}$ (h) $\frac{4}{9}$ (i) $\frac{7}{15}$
2 (a) $\frac{3}{10}$ (b) $\frac{7}{10}$
3 (a) $\frac{3}{8}$ shaded, $\frac{5}{8}$ unshaded
   (b) $\frac{8}{13}$ shaded, $\frac{5}{13}$ unshaded
   (c) $\frac{4}{9}$ shaded, $\frac{5}{9}$ unshaded
   (d) $\frac{7}{12}$ shaded, $\frac{5}{12}$ unshaded
4 (a) 17   (b) $\frac{10}{17}$ (c) $\frac{4}{17}$ (d) $\frac{3}{17}$ (e) $\frac{14}{17}$
5 (a) $\frac{2}{5}$ (b) $\frac{1}{4}$ (c) $\frac{2}{7}$ (d) $\frac{3}{5}$
   (e) $\frac{5}{6}$ (f) $\frac{7}{10}$ (g) $\frac{5}{8}$ (h) $\frac{11}{16}$
   (i) $\frac{13}{18}$ (j) $\frac{5}{8}$ (k) $\frac{7}{12}$ (l) $\frac{13}{18}$
6 (a) 14   (b) $\frac{7}{14}$ (c) $\frac{3}{14}$ (d) $\frac{13}{14}$
7 Pupils' drawings

Exercise 5.2

1 (a) $\frac{1}{2}=\frac{2}{4}$ (b) $\frac{1}{2}=\frac{4}{8}$ (c) $\frac{2}{6}=\frac{1}{3}$
   (d) $\frac{3}{4}=\frac{6}{8}$ (e) $\frac{2}{3}=\frac{6}{9}$ (f) $\frac{3}{5}=\frac{6}{10}$
2 Pupils' drawings
3 (d) $\frac{6}{8}$ (e) $\frac{2}{8}$ (f) $\frac{2}{8}$ (g) $\frac{10}{12}$
   (h) $\frac{6}{10}$ (i) $\frac{14}{16}$ (j) $\frac{12}{18}$

Exercise 5.3

1 (a) $\frac{4}{8}$ (b) ×5   (c) ×4, ×4
   (d) $\frac{2}{8}$ (e) $\frac{6}{15}$ (f) $\frac{5}{10}$
   (g) $\frac{4}{12}$ (h) $\frac{4}{8}$ (i) $\frac{4}{8}$
   (j) $\frac{1}{5}$, ×4   (k) $\frac{1}{2}$, ×2, $\frac{2}{4}$ (l) $\frac{1}{5}$, ×3
   (m) $\frac{1}{5}$, ×5   (n) $\frac{3}{3}$, ×4   (o) $\frac{3}{4}$, ×6, $\frac{18}{24}$
2 (a) $\frac{4}{8}$ (b) $\frac{4}{12}$ (c) $\frac{5}{20}$ (d) $\frac{4}{20}$
   (e) $\frac{7}{21}$ (f) $\frac{4}{6}$ (g) $\frac{3}{5}$ (h) $\frac{7}{8}$
   (i) $\frac{6}{7}$ (j) $\frac{13}{14}$

Exercise 5.4

1 (a) 5p   (b) 15 g   (c) 4€   (d) 6 ml
   (e) £12   (f) 9 cm   (g) £12   (h) 3 m
   (i) $2   (j) £4   (k) 12p   (l) £25
   (m) 2 litres   (n) 12€   (o) £1.50   (p) 7·5 mm
2 (a) 15 kg   (b) 34 g   (c) 41 ml   (d) 200p
   (e) £32   (f) 100   (g) 110 m   (h) 22p
   (i) £109   (j) 4 kg   (k) 60   (l) £2.50
3 10

Exercise 5.5

1 (a) 0·125   (b) 0·1   (c) 0·05   (d) 0·01
   (e) 0·75   (f) 0·8   (g) 0·625   (h) 0·7
   (i) 0·375   (j) 0·05   (k) 0·025   (l) 0·9
   (m) 0·3   (n) 0·35   (o) 0·425   (p) 0·333
2 0·5, 0·75, 0·2, 0·4, 0·6, 0·8, 0·1
3 Pupils' own work
4 $\frac{1}{2}=0·5$, $\frac{1}{4}=0·25$, $\frac{1}{5}=0·2$, $\frac{1}{8}=0·125$, $\frac{1}{10}=0·1$, $\frac{1}{20}=0·05$, $\frac{1}{100}=0·01$

Review Exercise 5

1 $\frac{3}{7}$
2 (a) 12   (b) $\frac{5}{12}$ (c) $\frac{7}{12}$
3 Pupils' answers
4 (a) $\frac{1}{3}=\frac{3}{9}$ (b) $\frac{3}{4}=\frac{6}{8}$
5 (a) $\frac{4}{8}$ (b) $\frac{6}{9}$ (c) $\frac{2}{5}$
6 (a) £10   (b) 8 kg   (c) 6 m   (d) £3.50
7 (a) 0·5   (b) 0·25   (c) 0·2
   (d) 0·125   (e) 0·4   (f) 0·95

Chapter 6

Exercise 6.1

1 (a) (b) (c)

(d) (e) (f)

(g) (h)

2 (a) (b) (c)

(d)

3 (a) 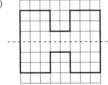 (b)

(c) 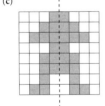 (d)

(e) 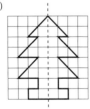 (f)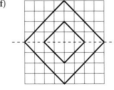

(g) 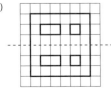 (h)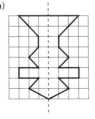

4 (a) 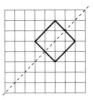 (b)

(c) (d)

(e) 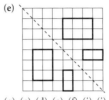 (f)

5 (a), (c), (d), (e), (f), (i), (j), (l)

6 (a) 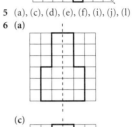 (b)

(c)

7 (a) 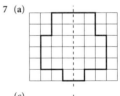 (b)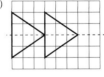

(c) (d)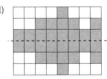

(e) 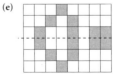 (f)

8 All except (a)

Exercise 6.2

1

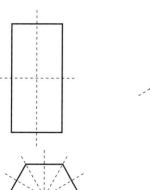
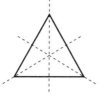

2 (a) none

(b)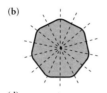

(c)

(d)

(e)

(f)

(g) none

(h)

(i) none

(j)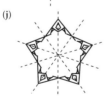

(k)

(l) none

3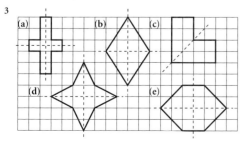

4 Albania: 1; France: 1; Laos: 2; Japan: 2; Switzerland: 2; Nigeria: 2;
   Vietnam: 1; Finland: 1

5 (a) 1   (b) 0   (c) 2   (d) 2
   (e) 1   (f) 2   (g) 4   (h) 1

6 (a) 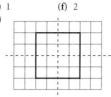   (b)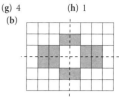

Exercise 6.3

1 (a) Yes   (b) Yes   (c) No   (d) No   (e) Yes
2 (a) and (b)
3 (b), (c), (e), (f), (g), (h)
4 H, I, O, S, X, Z
5 Micronesia, Nigeria, United Kingdom, Georgia
6 Pupils' answers
7 (a) 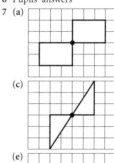   (b)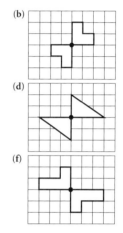

   (c)   (d)

   (e) 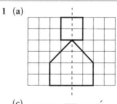   (f)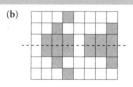

Exercise 6.4

1-5 Pupils' answers
6 (a) No, two circles next to each other only touch at one point. There
       would be gaps between the tiles.
   (b) No, exterior angles do not match interior angles.
7 Pupils' drawings

Review Exercise 6

1 (a)   (b)

   (c)   (d)

2 (a)   (b)   (c)

3 (a) 4   (b) 1   (c) 1   (d) 3
   (e) 1   (f) 2   (g) 2   (h) 0
4 (a), (b), (c), (d), (e), (h)
5 Pupils' drawings

Chapter 7

Exercise 7.1

1 (a) $\frac{90}{100}$, 90%   (b) $\frac{75}{100}$, 75%   (c) $\frac{10}{100}$, 10%
(d) $\frac{39}{100}$, 39%   (e) $\frac{42}{100}$, 42%   (f) $\frac{87}{100}$, 87%
(g) $\frac{67}{100}$, 67%   (h) $\frac{55}{100}$, 55%   (i) $\frac{91}{100}$, 91%

2

3 Pupils' drawings
4 (a) 14%   (b) 36%   (c) 87%   (d) 63%
(e) 51%   (f) 29%   (g) 91%   (h) 33%
(i) 99%   (j) 17%   (k) 10%   (l) 50%
5 (a) $\frac{23}{100}$ (b) $\frac{37}{100}$ (c) $\frac{63}{100}$ (d) $\frac{89}{100}$
(e) $\frac{11}{100}$ (f) $\frac{53}{100}$ (g) $\frac{67}{100}$ (h) $\frac{27}{100}$
(i) $\frac{99}{100}$ (j) $\frac{19}{100}$ (k) $\frac{1}{100}$ (l) $\frac{9}{100}$

Exercise 7.2

1 (a) £30   (b) 12 kg   (c) 150p
(d) £10   (e) 4 cm   (f) 8 ml
(g) £3   (h) 7 g   (i) 60p
2 (a) £45   (b) 20 kg   (c) 25p
(d) £16   (e) 16 m   (f) 18 ?
(g) £30   (h) 15 kg   (i) £1.50
3 (a) £20   (b) £21   (c) £27

Exercise 7.3

1 (a) 0·41   (b) 0·57   (c) 0·81   (d) 0·77
(e) 0·99   (f) 0·13   (g) 0·16   (h) 0·82
(i) 0·28   (j) 0·38   (k) 0·44   (l) 1·00
2 (a) 0·01   (b) 0·02   (c) 0·03
(d) 0·04   (e) 0·05   (f) 0·06
(g) 0·07   (h) 0·08   (i) 0·09
3 (a) 0·1   (b) 0·2   (c) 0·3
(d) 0·4   (e) 0·5   (f) 0·6
(g) 0·7   (h) 0·8   (i) 0·9

Exercise 7.4

1 (a) £85   (b) £160   (c) 70 kg
(d) 128 cm   (e) £64   (f) 420 g
(g) 84p   (h) 510 m   (i) 2970 km
2 (a) £14   (b) £30   (c) 6 g
(d) 25·6 kg   (e) £18   (f) 45 mm
(g) $40   (h) 26€   (i) £30
3 (a) £9.50   (b) £21.60   (c) £112.50
(d) £79.20   (e) £954.80
4 £62.50
5 60p
6 £20.50
7 £150
8 (a) £160   (b) £40
9 (a) £24   (b) £56
10 (a) £5.50   (b) £16.50   (c) £14.85

Review Exercise 7

1 (a) $\frac{39}{100}$ (b) 39%   (c) 61%
2 (a) 33%   (b) 91%   (c) 70%   (d) 3%
3 (a) $\frac{23}{100}$ (b) $\frac{71}{100}$ (c) $\frac{80}{100}$ (d) $\frac{9}{100}$
4 (a) £12   (b) 8 kg   (c) 60 m   (d) £1.50
5 £93.75
6 (a) 0·47   (b) 0·87   (c) 0·40   (d) 0·03
7 (a) £112   (b) 36 kg

Chapter 8

Exercise 8.1

1 (a)

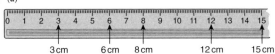

3 cm   6 cm   8 cm   12 cm   15 cm

(b)

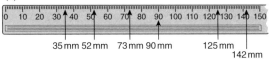

35 mm   52 mm   73 mm   90 mm   125 mm   142 mm

(c)

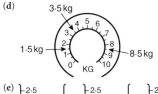

2 kg   5 kg   7 kg

(d)

3·5 kg   1·5 kg   8·5 kg

(e)

2 ℓ   1·5 ℓ   0·5 ℓ   0·75 ℓ

2 (a) 1 cm
(b) (i) 1 cm   (ii) 4 cm   (iii) 8 cm
(iv) 12 cm   (v) 14 cm
3 (a) 1 mm
(b) (i) 12 mm   (ii) 45 mm   (iii) 64 mm
(iv) 102 mm   (v) 136 mm
4 (a) 1 °C
(b) (i) 2 °C   (ii) 6 °C   (iii) 13 °C
(iv) 16 °C   (v) 21 °C
5 (a) 2 kg
(b) (i) 2 kg   (ii) 6 kg   (iii) 18 kg
(iv) 24 kg   (v) 28 kg
6 (a) 10 ml
(b) (i) 50 ml   (ii) 80 ml   (iii) 120 ml
(iv) 190 ml   (v) 230 ml
7 (a) 50 ml
(b) (i) 100 ml   (ii) 400 ml   (iii) 600 ml
(iv) 900 ml   (v) 1200 ml

Exercise 8.2

1 c, e, a, f, b, d
2 a, c, d, b, e, f
3 Pupils' answers
4 (i) 4 cm   (ii) 3 cm   (iii) 2 cm

Exercise 8.3

1 (i) 3 cm 6 mm = 3·6 cm = 36 mm
(ii) 6 cm 6 cm = 6·6 cm = 66 mm
(iii) 4 cm 8 mm = 4·8 cm = 48 mm
(iv) 2 cm 4 mm = 2·4 cm = 24 mm
(v) 6 cm 0 mm = 6·0 cm = 60 mm
2 2·4 cm, 3·6 cm, 4·8 cm, 6·0 cm, 6·6 cm
3 (a) 3·2 cm, 4·5 cm, 5·4 cm, 6·1 cm
(b) 49 mm, 53 mm, 67 mm, 81 mm
(c) 3·1 cm, 3·5 cm, 3·7 cm, 3·8 cm
(d) 90 mm, 91 mm, 95 mm, 99 mm

4 (i) 4 cm 5 mm = 4·5 cm = 45 mm
  (ii) 4 cm 2 mm = 4·2 cm = 42 mm
  (iii) 4 cm 8 mm = 4·8 cm = 48 mm
  (iv) 4 cm 9 mm = 4·9 cm = 49 mm
  (v) 4 cm 7 mm = 4·7 cm = 47 mm
5 (a) 2·5 cm **(b)** 3·4 cm **(c)** 6·2 cm **(d)** 8·7 cm
  (e) 9·9 cm **(f)** 3·5 cm **(g)** 2·8 cm **(h)** 0·5 cm
6 (a) 53 mm **(b)** 21 mm **(c)** 68 mm **(d)** 73 mm
  (e) 8 mm **(f)** 98 mm **(g)** 59 mm **(h)** 86 mm

Exercise 8.4

1 (a) (i) 1 m 48 cm, 1 m 88 cm
    (ii) 1·48 m, 1·88 m
    (iii) 148 cm, 188 cm
  (b) 1·8 m, 1·73 m, 1·88 m
2 (a) 1·4 m, 2·5 m, 3·4 m, 6·1 m
  (b) 4·56 m, 4·65 m, 4·76 m, 4·91 m
  (c) 560 cm, 568 cm, 569 cm, 580 cm
  (d) 7·1 m, 7·19 m, 7·9 m, 7·91 m
3 (a) 3·56 m, 5·3 m, 4·32 m, 2·5 m, 3·59 m
  (b) 2·5 m, 3·56 m, 3·59 m, 4·32 m, 5·3 m
4 (a) 3·45 m **(b)** 2·65 m **(c)** 7·13 m **(d)** 4·05 m
  (e) 2·5 m **(f)** 3·25 m **(g)** 2·06 m **(h)** 0·5 m
5 (a) 500 cm **(b)** 265 cm **(c)** 431 cm **(d)** 750 cm
  (e) 450 cm **(f)** 360 cm **(g)** 956 cm **(h)** 608 cm
6 3m 37 cm, 324 cm, 3m 16 cm, 3·09 m

Exercise 8.5

1 (i) 1m 500 mm = 1500 mm = 1·5 m
  (ii) 1m 750 mm = 1750 mm = 1·75 m
  (iii) 1m 250 mm = 1250 mm = 1·25 m
  (iv) 2m 0 mm = 2000 mm = 2 m
2 1·25 m, 1·5 m, 1·75 m, 2 m
3 (a) 4 m **(b)** 7 m **(c)** 5 m **(d)** 0·5 m
  (e) 2·5 m **(f)** 8·25 m **(g)** 5·75 m **(h)** 4·5 m
4 (a) 6000 mm **(b)** 4000 mm **(c)** 11 000 mm **(d)** 10 000 mm
  (e) 3500 mm **(f)** 6500 mm **(g)** 4750 mm **(h)** 500 mm
5 (a) Car Park: 3 km; Lochan: 4 km; Taigh Mor: 1·75 km;
    Cairn: 1·5 km ; Knock Hill: 2·5 km
  (b) 4 km, 3 km, 2·5 km, 1·75 km, 1·5 km
6 (a) 4 km **(b)** 6 km **(c)** 2·5 km **(d)** 0·25 km
7 (a) 3000 m **(b)** 8250 m **(c)** 2500 m **(d)** 8750 m

Exercise 8.6

1 Pupils' answers
2 (a) 40 kilogrammes **(b)** 1 tonne
  (c) 1 kilogramme **(d)** 100 grammes
3 (a) grammes **(b)** kilogrammes
  (c) grammes **(d)** kilogrammes
  (e) tonnes

Exercise 8.7

1 (a) 1 kg **(b)** 3 kg **(c)** 0·5 kg **(d)** 2·5 kg
2 1000 g, 3000 g, 500 g, 2500 g
3 (a) 5 kg **(b)** 2·5 kg **(c)** 3·5 kg **(d)** 0·5 kg
4 (a) 7000 g **(b)** 9500 g **(c)** 4500 g **(d)** 2750 g
5 (a) 6 kg 500 g **(b)** 7 kg 500 g **(c)** 10 kg 500 g **(d)** 3 kg 750 g
6 (i) 6 tonnes 400 kg = 6·4 tonnes
  (ii) 5 tonnes 400 kg = 5·4 tonnes
  (iii) 4 tonnes 500 kg = 4·5 tonnes
  (iv) 10 tonnes 600 kg = 10·6 tonnes
  (v) 77 tonnes 100 kg = 77·1 tonnes
  (vi) 136 tonnes 0 kg = 136 tonnes
7 Ultrasaurus, Brachiosaurus, Diplodocus, Tyrannosaurus,
  Triceratops, Iguanodon
8 (a) 5 tonnes **(b)** 6·5 tonnes **(c)** 2·5 tonnes **(d)** 3·5 tonnes
9 (a) 4 tonnes 600 kg **(b)** 7 tonnes 500 kg
  (c) 8 tonnes 721 kg **(d)** 3 tonnes 250 kg

Exercise 8.8

1 (a) 1 ℓ 0 ml **(b)** 2 ℓ 500 ml **(c)** 1 ℓ 750 ml **(d)** 1 ℓ 350 ml
2 1 ℓ 0 ml, 1 ℓ 350 ml, 1 ℓ 750 ml, 2 ℓ 500 ml
3 (a) 8 ℓ **(b)** 3·5 ℓ **(c)** 11 ℓ **(d)** 25 ℓ
  (e) 7·5 ℓ **(f)** 2·5 ℓ **(g)** 6·5 ℓ **(h)** 0·5 ℓ
4 (a) 7 ℓ 500 ml **(b)** 3 ℓ 500 ml **(c)** 5 ℓ 500 ml **(d)** 10 ℓ 500 ml
  (e) 3 ℓ 0 ml **(f)** 1 ℓ 500 ml **(g)** 1 ℓ 250 ml **(h)** 0ℓ 500 ml
5 (a) 4000 ml **(b)** 6500 ml **(c)** 8500 ml **(d)** 9750 ml
  (e) 1500 ml **(f)** 8500 ml **(g)** 3250 ml **(h)** 2750 ml

Exercise 8.9

1 (a) 4 m 25 cm **(b)** 5 m **(c)** 6 m 25 cm **(d)** 8 m 75 cm
2 (a) Pupils' drawings **(b)** 20 cm
3 Dens Park: 334 m; Tynecastle Stadium: 332·02 m; Pittodrie Stadium:
  333·86 m; Caledonian Stadium: 344·54 m; Victoria Park: 321·02 m
4 (a) 18 cm **(b)** 10 cm
5 Pupils' own work
6 (a) 8 km **(b)** 4·25 km **(c)** 7 km **(d)** 13 km
7 (a) 1·5 ℓ **(b)** 2 ℓ **(c)** 1·75 ℓ
8 73 kg
9 (a) 2·5 kg **(b)** 4·75 kg
10 1·1 m

Exercise 8.10

1 (a) 7 tonnes 500 kg **(b)** 12 tonnes 500 kg **(c)** 17 tonnes 500 kg
  (d) 22 tonnes 500 kg **(e)** 25 tonnes
2 (a) 14 m **(b)** 17 m 50 cm **(c)** 28 m
  (d) 31 m 50 cm **(e)** 35 m
3 (a) 0·3 ℓ **(b)** 0·375 ℓ **(c)** 0·25 ℓ **(d)** 0·15 ℓ
4 (a) 0·9 m **(b)** 0·6 m **(c)** 0·4 m **(d)** 0·72 m

Review Exercise 8

1 (a) 1 cm **(b)** 3 cm, 6 cm, 12 cm
2 (a) 1 °C **(b)** 2 °C, 7 °C, 13 °C
3 (b) 1·8 cm
4 (a) 3·5 cm **(b)** 2·7 cm **(c)** 5·3 cm **(d)** 4·2 cm
5 (a) 62 mm **(b)** 37 mm **(c)** 79 mm **(d)** 54 mm
6 (a) 5·65 m **(b)** 4·25 m **(c)** 2·5 m **(d)** 3·75 m
7 (a) 600 cm **(b)** 753 cm **(c)** 695 cm **(d)** 350 cm
8 (a) 8 m **(b)** 9·5 m **(c)** 7·5 m **(d)** 1·5 m
9 (a) 7000 mm **(b)** 3500 mm **(c)** 2500 mm **(d)** 12 000 mm
10 (a) 6 kg **(b)** 9·5 kg **(c)** 4·5 kg **(d)** 2·5 kg
11 (a) 8000 g **(b)** 5500 g **(c)** 3500 g **(d)** 6750 g
12 (a) 5 kg 500 g **(b)** 7 kg 500 g **(c)** 3 kg 750 g **(d)** 10 kg 500 g
13 (a) 6 ℓ **(b)** 8·5 ℓ **(c)** 12 ℓ **(d)** 6·5 ℓ
14 (a) 6 ℓ 500 ml **(b)** 2 ℓ 500 ml **(c)** 9 ℓ 500 ml **(d)** 1 ℓ 250 ml
15 (a) 6000 ml **(b)** 7500 ml **(c)** 3500 ml **(d)** 5750 ml
16 (a) 3·75 m **(b)** 6 m
17 (a) 1250 g **(b)** 3 kg 250 g
18 (a) 7·5 ℓ **(b)** 10·5 ℓ **(c)** 13·5 ℓ **(d)** 15 ℓ
19 (a) 40 g **(b)** 100 g **(c)** 300 g **(d)** 500 g

Chapter 9

Exercise 9.1

1 Pupils' drawings
2 Pupils' drawings
3 (a) 7:30 **(b)** 9:45 **(c)** 10:50
  (d) 1:45 **(e)** 4:25 **(f)** 1:50
  (g) 6:35 **(h)** 12:30 **(i)** 2:40
4 (a) twenty past ten **(b)** 3 o'clock
  (c) five past four **(d)** quarter to two
  (e) twenty-five past seven **(f)** half past six
5 (a) twenty past eleven **(b)** quarter past six
  (c) twenty-five to three **(d)** five past nine
  (e) twelve o'clock **(f)** five o'clock
  (g) five to five **(h)** three minutes past three
  (i) one minute past ten

6 (a) 9.05   (b) 2.15   (c) 6.30
   (d) 6.50   (e) 11.35   (f) 11.20

Exercise 9.2

1 (a) 6.30 p.m.   (b) 4.15 p.m.   (c) 1.45 a.m.
   (d) 1.10 p.m.   (e) 7.30 p.m.   (f) 7.45 a.m.
2 (a) 6.30 p.m. (b) 3.15 p.m. (c) 10.50 a.m. (d) 11.15 p.m.
   (e) 3.40 a.m. (f) 8.25 p.m. (g) 10.30 a.m. (h) 12.00 p.m.
   (i) 7.45 a.m. (j) 12.00 a.m.
3 (a) 7.30 a.m.   (b) 1.30 p.m.   (c) 2.15 p.m.
   (d) 10.30 p.m.   (e) 11.10 p.m.   (f) 4.30 p.m.
   (g) 7.45 a.m.   (h) 11.20 a.m.   (i) 9.30 p.m.

Exercise 9.3

1 (a) 08 15   (b) 18 30   (c) 19 15   (d) 02 15
   (e) 10 20   (f) 11 08   (g) 20 06   (h) 21 10
   (i) 23 09   (j) 02 20   (k) 05 35   (l) 19 28
   (m) 18 40   (n) 05 50   (o) 09 25   (p) 02 45
   (q) 23 45   (r) 01 22   (s) 11 11   (t) 13 05
2 12.40 a.m. = 00 40; 7.35 a.m. = 07 35; 1.05 p.m. = 13 05;
   midnight = 00 00
   20 06 = 8.06 p.m.; 22 55 = 10.55 p.m.; 12 00 = noon;
   13 10 = 1.10 p.m.; 17 20 = 5.20 p.m.
3 Glasgow 08 00, Edinburgh 09 30, Newcastle 12 15, Durham 15 20,
   York 19 54
4 4.30 a.m. = 04 30; 2.15 p.m. = 14 15; 5.35 p.m. = 17 35;
   3.05 a.m. = 03 05; 9.10 p.m. = 21 10
5 (c)
6 LFH519
7 No
8 (a) 4.10 p.m.   (b) 9.30 p.m.   (c) 9.15 a.m.   (d) 2.20 a.m.
   (e) 10.08 a.m. (f) 5.05 p.m.   (g) 10.00 p.m. (h) 3.30 a.m.
   (i) 6.35 a.m.   (j) 1.45 p.m.   (k) 6.55 p.m.   (l) 2.10 p.m.
   (m) 11.30 p.m. (n) 2.25 a.m.   (o) 8.17 p.m.   (p) 5.55 a.m.
   (q) 12.00 p.m. (noon)   (r) 4.12 a.m.   (s) 12.15 a.m.
   (t) 12.20 a.m.
9 16 15 = 4.15 p.m.; 05 20 = 5.20 a.m.; 21 12 = 9.12 p.m.;
   20 40 = 8.40 p.m.
   8.40 p.m. = 20 40; 1.01 a.m. = 01 01; 1.35 p.m. = 13 35;
   midnight = 00 00; 11 p.m. = 23 00
10 Hamburg: 9.15 a.m.; Lubeck: 11.20 a.m.; Rostock: 1.05 p.m.;
    Stralsund: 2.25 p.m.
11 Yes, as it is five minutes past 16 30, which is his finishing time.
12 Yes, as that is twenty-five minutes before 17 15.
13 21 21 = 9:21 p.m.; 22 00 = 10 p.m.; 12 10 = 12:10 p.m.;
    07 05 = 7:05 a.m.; 8 a.m. = 08 00; 3:15 p.m. = 15 15;
    16 30 = 4:30 p.m.; 11:15 p.m. = 23 15; 1:10 a.m. = 01 10;
    19 05 = 7:05 p.m.; 04 30 = 4:30 a.m.; 10:15 a.m. = 10 15

Exercise 9.4

1 (a) Phil   (b) George   (c) Drew
2 Blackie
3 (a) Stan   (b) Pete   (c) Bill
4 (a) Barry   (b) Sara
5 (a) Mel   (b) Mel, Paul, Brad, Steve, Denzil
   (c) Mel, Paul

Exercise 9.5

1 (a) 33 mins   (b) 12 mins   (c) 27 mins
2 (a) 1 hr 10 mins (b) 1 hr 15 mins (c) 1 hr 19 mins
   (d) 1 hr 50 mins (e) 1 hr 25 mins (f) 2 hrs 40 mins
3 Newsday: 45 mins; Westenders: 50 mins; Republic St: 35 mins;
   Showtime: 45 mins
4 A: 35 mins; B: 30 mins; C: 40 mins; D: 45 mins
5 (a) 8 hrs 35 mins (b) 2 hrs   (c) 3 hrs 10 mins
   (d) 1 hr 30 mins (e) 2 hrs 40 mins
6 8hrs 45 mins
7 4 hrs 45 mins

Review Exercise 9

1 (a) ten past nine   (b) twenty-five to four
   (c) twenty to ten
2 (a) five past five   (b) ten to eleven
   (c) quarter to ten
3 (a) 5.50 p.m. (b) 4.30 a.m. (c) 8.20 p.m. (d) 12 p.m.
4 (a) 07 00   (b) 12 20   (c) 18 30   (d) 02 15
5 2.25 p.m. = 14 25; 4.30 p.m. = 16 30; 9.15 a.m. = 09 15;
   10.05 p.m. = 22 05; 1.20 p.m. = 13 20; 3.05 a.m. = 03 05
6 Yes. 16 45 = 4.45 + 35 = 5.20 p.m.
7 (a) Sara   (b) Sakina
8 (a) Lap 1: 1 hr 13 mins, Lap 2: 1 hr 29 mins, Lap 3: 2 hrs 24 mins
   (b) Lap 1
9 6 hrs 45 mins

Chapter 10

Exercise 10.1

1 (a) 12 cm   (b) 18 cm   (c) 18 cm
   (d) 14 cm   (e) 20 cm   (f) 20 cm
2 (a) 8 cm   (b) 14 cm   (c) 12 cm
   (d) 12 cm   (e) 16 cm   (f) 14 cm
3 (a) 14 cm (b) 14 cm (c) 16 cm (d) 14 cm
   (e) 12 cm (f) 12 cm (g) 14 cm (h) 18 cm
   (i) 12 cm (j) 14 cm (k) 14 cm (l) 24 cm
4 (a) 12 cm (b) 30 mm (c) 9 m (d) 8 cm
   (e) 14 m (f) 11 cm (g) 24 cm (h) 25 m
   (i) 34 cm (j) 9 m
5 (a) Bottom Meadow: 140 m, High Park: 133 m, Curlew Land: 160 m
   (b) Curlew Land
   (c) £70

Exercise 10.2

1 (a) $4 \times 2 = 8$ cm^2 (b) $5 \times 3 = 15$ cm^2
   (c) $5 \times 4 = 20$ cm^2 (d) $6 \times 1 = 6$ cm^2
   (e) $7 \times 3 = 21$ cm^2 (f) $5 \times 5 = 25$ cm^2
   (g) $12 \times 2 = 24$ cm^2
2 (a) 6 cm^2 (b) 15 cm^2 (c) 4 cm^2
   (d) 4 cm^2 (e) 10 cm^2 (f) 9 cm^2
   (g) 18 cm^2 (h) 16 cm^2 (i) 7 cm^2
3 (a) Perimeter = 14 cm, Area = 10 cm^2
   (b) Perimeter = 16 cm, Area = 16 cm^2
   (c) Perimeter = 12 cm, Area = 5 cm^2
   (d) Perimeter = 12 cm, Area = 8 cm^2
   (e) Perimeter = 18 cm, Area = 20 cm^2
   (f) Perimeter = 12 cm, Area = 9 cm^2
4 (a) 12 cm   (b) 15 cm   (c) 12 cm

Exercise 10.3

1 (a) $8\frac{1}{2}$ cm^2 (b) 7 cm^2 (c) $8\frac{1}{2}$ cm^2
   (d) 4 cm^2 (e) 8 cm^2 (f) 12 cm^2
   (g) $10\frac{1}{2}$ cm^2 (h) $8\frac{1}{2}$ cm^2 (i) 8 cm^2

Exercise 10.4

1 (a) 4 cm^2 (b) 2 cm^2 (c) 8 cm^2
   (d) 12 cm^2 (e) 10 cm^2 (f) $4\frac{1}{2}$ cm^2

Exercise 10.5

1 (a) 16 square units
   (b) 14 square units
   (c) 12 square units
   (d) 8 square units
   (e) 9 square units
   (f) 21 square units

2 (a)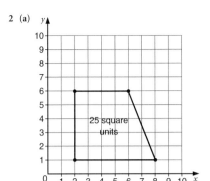

(b)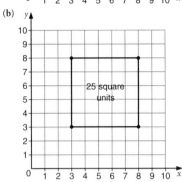

(c)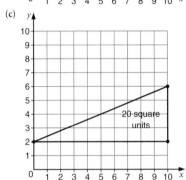

(d)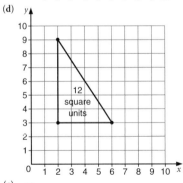

(e)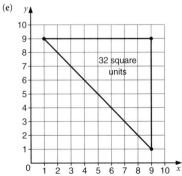

(f)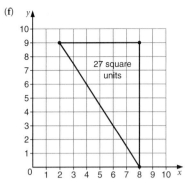

3 (a) 99 m² **(b)** 81 m² **(c)** 36 m²
4 (a) 48 m² **(b)** 36 m² **(c)** 50 m²
(d) 24 m² **(e)** 22.5 m²
5 (a) (i) 15 m² **(ii)** 26 m² **(iii)** 12.5 m²
(b) Kitchen floor
(c) £117

Exercise 10.6

1 (a) A = 10 cm², B = 1 cm², Total = 11 cm²
(b) K = 6 cm², L = 6 cm², Total = 12 cm²
(c) F = 12 cm², G = 4 cm², Total = 16 cm²
(d) P = 4 cm², Q = 2 cm², Total = 6 cm²
(e) X = 4 cm², Y = 3 cm², Total = 7 cm²
(f) D = 9 cm², F = 3 cm², Total = 12 cm²
(g) R = 16 cm², T = 3 cm², Total = 19 cm²
2 (a) 32 cm² **(b)** 23 cm² **(c)** 22 cm²
3 (a) Lounge: 72 m²; Kitchen: 25 m²; Conservatory: 10 m²
(b) 107 m²
(c) £1070

Review Exercise 10

1 (a) 16 cm **(b)** 20 cm **(c)** 14 cm
2 (a) 12 cm **(b)** 16 cm **(c)** 16 cm
3 (a) 27 cm² **(b)** 49 cm² **(c)** 40 cm²
4 (a) 10 cm² **(b)** 10 cm² **(c)** 8 cm²
5 (a) 20 cm² **(b)** 14 cm² **(c)** 10·5 cm²
6

7 (a) 41 m² **(b)** £4.10
8 62 cm²

Chapter 11

Exercise 11.1

1 (a) (i) 2 **(ii)** 5 **(iii)** 7 **(iv)** 6
(b) size 6
2 (a) Football **(b)** Tennis **(c)** 10
(d) Golf **(e)** 58
3 (a) Italy **(b)** 16 **(c)** Turkey **(d)** USA
4 Orange
5 Seasand
6 1100
7 2ply

8

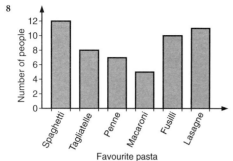

9

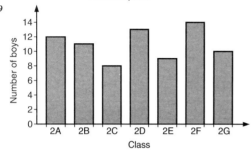

10

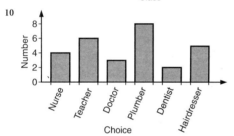

6

7

8

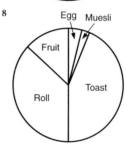

9 Fusilli, Penne, Ravioli, Lasagne, Spaghetti

Exercise 11.2

1 (a) 8°C   (b) 10 a.m.   (c) 2°C at 8 a.m.

2 (a) £15   (b) March   (c) December
   (d) April   (e) £10   (f) Fell by £25

3 (a) 60   (b) Week 4   (c) Week 6
   (d) 30   (e) 30
   4. 10 a.m.; 12 p.m. (noon)
   5. Tuesday; Wednesday and Thursday
   6. Wednesday; Friday, as it had the lowest attendance.
   7. Week 5

4 (a) 2003   (b) 2001 and 2002   (c) 2003 and 2004

5 (a) 12 and 13
   (b) No, because she appears to have stopped growing at 147 cm.

6 (a) 2003   (b) 2003 and 2005   (c) More common

Exercise 11.3

1 (a) Dogs   (b) Budgies   (c) Yes   (d) False

2 (a) Spain   (b) No
   (c) Spain, Italy, Britain, Canada, USA

3 (a) Maths   (b) Science, French   (c) Music, Art, PE

4 (a) Money   (b) Parents
   (c) Parents, children, health, crime, work, money

5

Exercise 11.4

1 (a) 125 cm, 52 kg   (b) 130 cm, 58 kg   (c) 120 cm, 54 kg
   (d) 140 cm, 57 kg   (e) 145 cm, 59 kg

2 (a) 11
   (b) 36
   (c) 37
   (d) 12
   (e) Yes as a general pattern, as the points are higher on the right.

3 (a) 120 cm
   (b) 18 cm
   (c) John
   (d) 125 cm
   (e) 24 cm
   (f) Yes as a general pattern, as the points are higher on the right.
   (g) 7

4 (a) 58 kg
   (b) Hazel
   (c) 54 kg
   (d) Sam
   (e) 62 kg
   (f) Blue
   (g) No, as the points show no clear pattern.

5

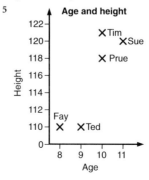

6

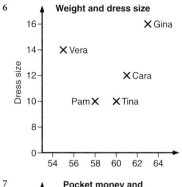

Weight and dress size

7

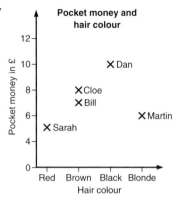

Pocket money and hair colour

8

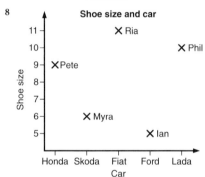

Shoe size and car

1 (a) 4
   (b) Sussair
   (c) Delpha and Norair
   (d) Fastjet
   (e) 8

2

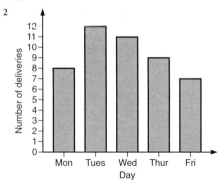

3 (a) 3
   (b) Wednesday
   (c) 5
   (d) 15

4

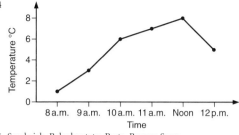

5 Sandwich, Baked potato, Pasta, Burger, Soup
6 (a) 13   (b) Grade 5
   (c) Frank   (d) 12
   (e) Grade 6   (f) Generally, yes.

Chapter 12

1 (a) 18, 20, 22; Add 2
   (b) 15, 18, 21; Add 3
   (c) 30, 25, 20; Subtract 5
   (d) 16, 14, 12; Subtract 2
   (e) 17, 21, 25; Add 4
   (f) 44, 54, 64; Add 10
   (g) 36, 45, 54; Add 9
   (h) 12, 6, 0; Subtract 6
   (i) 24, 19, 14; Subtract 5
   (j) 68, 60, 52; Subtract 8
   (k) 16, 32, 64; Multiply by 2
   (l) 27, 81, 243; Multiply by 3
   (m) 4, 2, 1; Divide by 2
   (n) 100, 10, 1; Divide by 10
   (o) $\frac{5}{6}, \frac{6}{7}, \frac{7}{8}$; Add 1 to both top and bottom
2 (a) 50, 51, 52, 53, 54, 55
   (b) 40, 36, 32, 28, 24, 20
   (c) 0, 9, 18, 27, 36, 45
   (d) 100, 90, 80, 70, 60, 50
   (e) 100, 200, 300, 400, 500, 600
   (f) $5\frac{1}{2}$, 5, $4\frac{1}{2}$, 4, $3\frac{1}{2}$, 3
   (g) 12·5, 10·5, 8·5, 6·5, 4·5, 2·5
3 1, 3, 5, 7, 9, 11, 13, 15, 17, 19
4 £64
5 (a) (i) 120, 110, 100, 90, 80, 70, 60, 50, 40, 30, 20, 10
       (ii) 1, 4, 7, 10, 13, 16, 19, 22, 25, 28, 31, 34
   (b) 10
6 (a) 15, 21   (b) 30, 42   (c) 25, 36
7 (a) 13, 21   (b) 18, 29   (c) 34, 55

1 (a) Pupils' artwork   (b) 4,6,8   (c) 2
   (d) 2   (e) (i) 14   (ii) 20
2 (a) 4   (b) 10, 15, 20   (c) 5   (d) 5
   (e) (i) 30   (ii) 60
3 (a) Pupils' artwork
   (b) 16, 24, 32
   (c) 8
   (d) 8
   (e) (i) 56   (ii) 80
4 (a) Pupils' artwork
   (b) 6, 12, 18, 24
   (c) 6
   (d) 6 times the number of chains
   (e) (i) 36   (ii) 60
5 (a) Pupils' drawings
   (b) 3, 6, 9, 12
   (c) 3
   (d) The number of men is 3 times the number of boats.
   (e) (i) 15 men   (ii) 27 men

Exercise 12.3

1 (a) Pupils' artwork   (b) 3, 6, 9, 12   (c) 3
    (d) 3   (e) 21
2 (a) Pupils' artwork   (b) 6, 12, 18, 24   (c) 6
    (d) 6   (e) 42
3 (a) Pupils' artwork   (b) 6, 12, 18, 24   (c) 6
    (d) 6   (e) 42
4 (a) Pupils' artwork   (b) 5, 10, 15, 20   (c) 5
    (d) 5   (e) 35
5 (a) The number of matches is 10 times the number of shapes;
      100 matches
   (b) The number of matches is 9 times the number of shapes;
      90 matches
   (c) The number of matches is 7 times the number of shapes;
      70 matches

Review Exercise 12

1 (a) 3, 8, 13, 18, 23, 28   (b) 40, 36, 32, 28, 24, 20
   (c) 1, 2, 4, 8, 16, 32   (d) $\frac{1}{2}$, 1, 1$\frac{1}{2}$, 2, 2$\frac{1}{2}$, 3
2 (a) 29, 36, 43   (b) 87, 84, 81
   (c) 54, 65, 76   (d) 58, 62, 66
3 (a) Sat evening: £36, Sun: £31, Mon: £26, Tues: £21, Weds: £16,
      Thurs: £11, Fri: £6 ($41 - 5n$)
   (b) £6
4 (a) Pupils' drawings   (b) 6, 12, 18, 24   (c) 6
    (d) six   (e) 42, 60
5 The number of matches is 6 times the number of shapes; 42 matches

Chapter 13

Exercise 13.1

1 (a) millimetre   (b) metre
   (c) centimetre   (d) kilometre
   (e) centimetre   (f) centimetre or metre
   (g) metre   (h) millimetre
   (i) centimetre   (j) kilometre
2 (a) 15 mm   (b) 22 mm   (c) 9 mm   (d) 41 mm
   (e) 3·3 cm   (f) 2·6 cm   (g) 58 mm   (i) 29 mm
   (j) 31 mm   (k) 44 mm
3 Pupils' answers
4 (a) 3 cm, 3 cm, 3 cm   (b) 2 cm, 5 cm, 5 cm, 2 cm
   (c) 2 cm, 5 cm, 3·5 cm, 2·5 cm   (d) 5 cm, 3 cm, 7 cm, 3 cm
5 (a) Pupils' drawings   (b) It is a square.
6 Pupils' drawings

Exercise 13.2

1 (a) right-angled   (b) isosceles
   (c) equilateral   (d) isosceles
   (e) scalene   (f) right-angled
2 (a) 4·3 cm, 3 cm, 3 cm; right-angled isosceles
   (b) 3 cm, 3 cm, 3 cm; equilateral
   (c) 3·5 cm, 4 cm, 4 cm; isosceles
   (d) 2·5 cm, 6 cm, 6 cm; isosceles
   (e) 4 cm, 3 cm, 3 cm; isosceles
   (f) 3 cm, 4 cm, 5 cm; right-angled
   (g) 4·5 cm, 4·5 cm, 3 cm; isosceles
   (h) 3·8 cm, 2 cm, 3·8 cm; isosceles
3 Pupils' drawings

Exercise 13.3

1-2 Pupils' drawings
3 (a) side: AD, diagonal: BD, angle: ∠ADC
   (b) side: IJ, diagonal: HJ, angle: ∠IHJ
   (c) side: MN, diagonal: MP, angle: ∠NOP
4 (a) side: HI, diagonal: FH, angle: ∠GFI
   (b) side: TU, diagonal: TV, angle: ∠TSV
   (c) side: CD, diagonal: AC, angle: ∠AED
5 Pupils' drawings

Exercise 13.4

1 (a) Rectangle   (b) Triangle
   (c) Pentagon   (d) Square
   (e) Hexagon   (f) Triangle
   (g) Triangle   (h) Pentagon
   (i) Rectangle   (j) Hexagon
   (k) Pentagon   (l) Square
2 (a-b)

   (c) 5
3 (a-b)

   (c) 9
4 Pupils' drawings

Exercise 13.5

1 Pupils' drawings
2 (a)

Circle	Radius	Diameter
A	21 mm	42 mm
B	10 mm	20 mm
C	25 mm	50 mm
D	15 mm	30 mm
E	23 mm	46 mm
F	35 mm	70 mm

   (b) double
3 (a) 8·4 cm   (b) 22 mm   (c) 7 m   (d) 40·2 cm
4 (a) 8 cm   (b) 12 mm   (c) 6·5 cm   (d) 60 m
5

Length of radius	4 cm	9 cm	11 m	4.5 cm	12 m	25 km	31 km
Length of diameter	8 cm	18 cm	22 m	9 cm	24 m	50 km	62 km

6 (a) radius: 11 cm, diameter: 22 cm
   (b) radius: 16 m, diameter: 32 m
7 (a) 20 cm   (b) 24·6 m   (c) 40 cm

Exercise 13.6

1-4 Pupils' drawings

Review Exercise 13

1 (a) centimetre   (b) millimetre
   (c) metre   (d) kilometre
2 (a) 29 mm   (b) 55 mm
3 Length: 65 mm, Width: 27 mm
4 Pupils' drawings
5 (a) 2right-angled   (b) equilateral   (c) isosceles
6 (a) AC   (b) DE   (c) ∠ABC
7 (a) D   (b) C
8 (a) red   (b) blue   (c) green
9 Pupils' drawings

Chapter 14

Exercise 14.1

1 (a) green/red   (b) Blackbird
2 (a) Brown   (b) Blue   (c) 2   (d) 5

3 (a) Stella:

Score	Tally	Frequency
3	JHT I	6
4	JHT I	6
5	JHT	5
6	I	1
7		0

Mode : 3 and 4

Gwen:

Score	Tally	Frequency
2	I	1
3	I	1
4	JHT	5
5	JHT III	7
6	III	3
7	I	1

Dana:

Score	Tally	Frequency
2		0
3		0
4	JHT I	6
5	JHT	5
6	JHT	5
7	II	2

(b) Stella: 3 or 4
Gwen: 5
Dana: 4

4 (a)

Goals	Tally	Frequency
0	II	2
1	JHT I	6
2	JHT IIII	9
3	II	2
4	I	1
5	I	1
6	I	1

(b) 2

Exercise 14.2

1 (a)

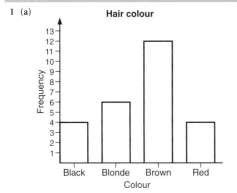

(b)

(c)

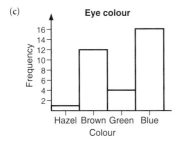

(d)

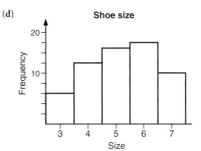

2 (a)

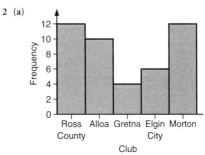

(b)

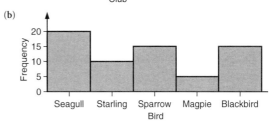

(c)

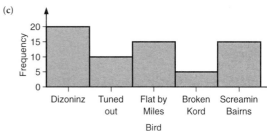

(d)

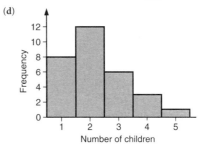

3 (a)

Colour	Tally	Frequency
Brown	JHT JHT IIII	14
Black	JHT JHT II	12
Blonde	JHT III	8
Red	JHT I	6

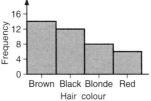

(b)

Goals	Tally	Frequency
0	III	3
1	II	2
2	JHT II	7
3	IIII	4
4	III	3
5	I	1

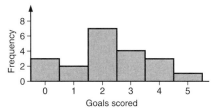

(c)

Size	Tally	Frequency
5	JHT II	7
6	JHT JHT IIII	14
7	JHT III	8
8	IIII	4
9	JHT	5
10	II	2

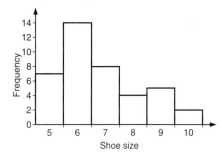

4-5 Pupils' work

Exercise 14.3

1 **(a)** Dog: 9; Cat: 7; Fish: 2; Hamster: 6; Guinea Pig: 3
   (b) Curry: 2; Pie: 4; Rice: 6; Chips: 8; Chicken: 6
   (c) BBC1: 15; BBC2: 5; ITV: 15; Ch4: 5; Ch5: 2
   (d) Football: 30; Rugby: 10; Tennis: 8; Hockey: 12; Athletics: 4

2 **(a)**

Travel	Frequency
Bike	4
Walk	9
Car	7
Bus	2

(b)

Goals	Frequency
1	4
2	6
3	6
4	2
5	1

(c)

Absences	Frequency
1	5
2	9
3	12
4	14
5	16

(d)

Pastime	Frequency
Sport	30
Games	26
TV	24
Reading	11
Shopping	28

Exercise 14.4

1 **(a)** 6   **(b)** 4   **(c)** 6   **(d)** 7
   (e) 5   **(f)** 4   **(g)** 5   **(h)** 5·6

2 **(a)** Round 1: 4·9, Round 2: 4·7
   (b) Round 2

3 **(a)** Waytown: 24, Erskine: 37·2
   (b) Erskine
   (c) Erskine, because it has more seagulls on average.

Review Exercise 14

1 **(a)**

Colour	Tally	Frequency
Black	JHT	5
Red	JHT	5
Yellow	JHT	5
Green	JHT I	6
Pink	IIII	4
Purple	JHT	5
Blue	JHT IIII	9
Brown	I	1

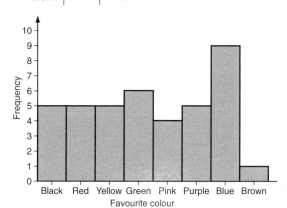

(b)

Number	Tally	Frequency
0	III	3
1	JHT III	8
2	JHT JHT	10
3	III	3
4	IIII	4
5	II	2

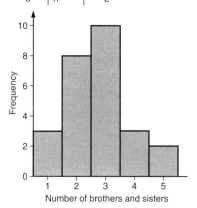

2 (a)

Music	Frequency
Folk	10
Rock	15
Pop	19
Classical	4
Indie	12

(b)

Drinks	Frequency
Cola	40
Orange	26
Water	38
Lemonade	50
Milk	16

3 (a) 6　　　　**(b)** 4　　　　**(c)** 6　　　　**(d)** 8

4 (a) First year: 4, Second year: 3　　**(b)** First year

Chapter 15

Exercise 15.1

1 (a) Sphere　　**(b)** Cuboid　　**(c)** Sphere
　(d) Pyramid　　**(e)** Cylinder　　**(f)** Cylinder
　(g) Cylinder　　**(h)** Cuboid　　**(i)** Cuboid
　(j) Triangular prism　**(k)** Cone　　**(l)** Cuboid
　(m) Triangular prism

2 (a) Vertex　**(b)** Face　**(c)** Edge　　**(d)** Edge
　(e) Vertex　**(f)** Face　**(g)** Vertex

3 Cube: vertices 8, edges 12, faces 6
　Cuboid: vertices 8, edges 12, faces 6

4 (a) vertices 5, edges 8, faces 5
　(b) vertices 6, edges 9, faces 5
　(c) vertices 12, edges 18, faces 8
　(d) vertices 6, edges 12, faces 8

Exercise 15.2

1

Number of edges	Length
4	7 cm
4	5 cm
4	4 cm

Number of vertices　8

2

Number of edges	Length
4	9 cm
4	5 cm
4	4 cm

Number of vertices　8

3

Number of edges	Length
4	8 cm
8	5 cm

Number of vertices　8

4

Number of edges	Length
12	6 cm

Number of vertices　8

5

Number of edges	Length
4	8 cm
4	4 cm

Number of vertices　5

6

Number of edges	Length
3	9 cm
6	5 cm

Number of vertices　6

Exercise 15.3

1-4 Pupils' work

Exercise 15.4

1

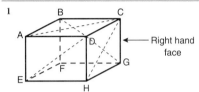
Right hand face

2

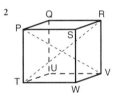

3

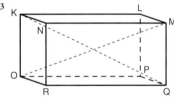

4 (a)

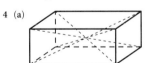

(b)

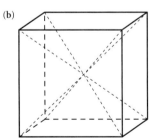

5 (a) JS and KM　　　　**(b)** RZ and SZ
6 (a) PV and RT　　　　**(b)** AG and BH
7 RT, SU and QW

Exercise 15.5

1 (a) ∠BHE　　　　**(b)** ∠UTV
2 (a) ∠OQS　　　　**(b)** ∠MQO
3 (a) red　　**(b)** blue　　**(c)** green
4 (a) ∠KMJ　　　　**(b)** ∠XCZ

Review Exercise 15

1 (**a**) Face   (**b**) Vertex   (**c**) Edge
2 (**a**) vertices 8, edges 12, faces 6
   (**b**) vertices 10, edges 15, faces 7
   (**c**) vertices 5, edges 8, faces 5
3 A = 3, B = 1, C = 2, D = 4
4 (**a**) AC and BD   (**b**) DG
5 (**a**) AG and BH   (**b**) EC
6 (**a**) ∠SRU   (**b**) ∠TZW

Chapter 16

1	Jon	Greg	Bina
	Jon	Anna	Bina
	Jon	Ben	Bina
	Jon	Greg	Jeff
	Jon	Anna	Jeff
	Jon	Ben	Jeff
	Jon	Greg	Rory
	Jon	Anna	Rory
	Jon	Ben	Rory
	Sanjay	Greg	Bina
	Sanjay	Anna	Bina
	Sanjay	Ben	Bina
	Sanjay	Greg	Jeff
	Sanjay	Anna	Jeff
	Sanjay	Ben	Jeff
	Sanjay	Greg	Rory
	Sanjay	Anna	Rory
	Sanjay	Ben	Rory	(18 teams)

2 (**a**) Taxi rank   (**b**) Bus station   (**c**) Chemist
3 (**a**) 12   (**b**) 8
4 Pupils' work
5 (**a**) [Shown on the diagram for (e)]
   (**b**)

   (**c**)

(**d**)

(**e**)

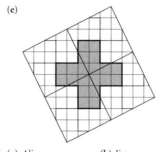

6 (**a**) Ali   (**b**) Jim   (**c**) Zoe
7 (**a**)

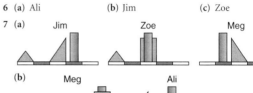

(**b**)

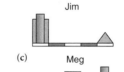

(**c**)

(**d**)

Index